CRACKING
—THE—
MARWARI CODE
Timeless Proverbs for Business Management

B.L. MITTAL

ISBN
Paperback 979-8-89673-801-5
Hardcase 979-8-89744-281-2

Copyright Disclaimer

This book is a work of non-fiction. While every effort has been made to ensure accuracy, the author and publisher do not assume and hereby disclaim any liability to any party for any loss, damage, or disruption caused by errors or omissions, whether such errors or omissions result from negligence, accident, or any other cause.

All rights reserved. No part of this publication may be reproduced, distributed or transmitted in any form or by any means, including photocopying, recording or other electronic or mechanical methods, without the prior written permission of the author or publisher, except in the case of brief quotations used in critical reviews and specific other non-commercial uses permitted by copyright law.

For permission requests, please contact the publisher at the address provided.

Who Should Read this Book?

- Startup founders

- SME (small and medium enterprises) leaders on the journey of founding or scaling their ventures

- Key managerial personnel or aspiring leaders aiming for senior management positions

- Young professionals stepping into management roles

- Business management students

- Knowledge seekers and lifelong learners looking to gain practical insights from the experiences of the Marwari community

Why this Book

The Marwari community has long been a *flagbearer* of entrepreneurship in India, cultivating a legacy of resilience and success. This book is neither a compilation of individual success stories nor a mere collection of data points. Instead, it is an endeavour to capture the essence of Marwari wisdom and values that have transformed the community from humble beginnings into one of India's *leading* entrepreneurial forces.

When a community consistently thrives in a particular field, there is often a deep-seated cultural heritage that drives this success – habits, values, and traditions that turn nothing into everything.

As India moves into its *Amrit Kaal* and strives to become a *Viksit Bharat* by 2047, aiming to be the world's third-largest economy within five years, a culture of entrepreneurship is essential. For any nation, including India, finding a development model rooted in its own culture can foster progress and inclusivity, allowing every citizen to contribute to this inspiring vision.

This book is an effort to distil the unique *desi formula* that has guided the Marwari community, as encapsulated in traditional one-line proverbs or *lokokti*. These age-old sayings hold practical wisdom, providing insights into values that can nurture entrepreneurship.

Beyond simply sharing these proverbs, this book reflects the personal experiences of the author, who has built his own entrepreneurial journey from scratch. Each chapter concludes with actionable takeaways, making it easier for readers to understand how even the simplest of greetings, like *Ram Ram sa* or *Haare ka sahara Baba Shyam hamara, Balaji ko aasro, Jai Jeen Maata*, contribute to a culture that fosters entrepreneurial spirit. Through this journey, we invite readers to reflect on the Marwari approach and discover how it may inspire their own path forward.

Preface

Before I go into the heart of this book, I feel it is important to share the why – the reason behind my desire to write.

Communities are often shaped by religion, caste, or language, and each one carries a unique strength that drives its progress. These strengths, over time, create habits that contribute to what I like to call the 'fragrance of development'.

To truly understand this fragrance and share its essence, we must first look at its roots – the community's way of living and working. Proverbs, for instance, are born from these roots. They are simple words carrying deep wisdom, passed down through generations, often with a story that tugs at your heart or leaves you reflecting for days.

But you may ask: why Marwari proverbs specifically? Because as a Marwari myself, I learnt early on from my father, the late Sanwar Mal Mittal, how our community has cultivated an ecosystem over the years where business and entrepreneurship thrive. There is just something special about this community that has had years of experience in this particular field, and those experiences manifest in ways that are subtle yet powerful.

In my own business journey, I have had the privilege of building two startups: one in investment banking and wealth management (Microsec) and another in digital healthcare (SastaSundar). Along the way, I have been fortunate to work closely with both Marwari and non-Marwari businesspeople. And I have always paid attention to the one-line proverbs that would come up in conversation. What struck me was how these simple phrases carried profound insights – insights that, in many ways, were already guiding my own entrepreneurial path.

I have actively listened to and collected those proverbs ever since, and now I feel compelled to share them, not just with the Marwari community but with society at large. Through this collection, I am honoured to illustrate how their wisdom has shaped my journey. I also aim to outline practical lessons and meaningful conclusions that can benefit you.

The core idea behind all these proverbs is simple: inclusive community participation lies at the heart of the Marwari community. This has been the bedrock of my own success as well. I grew up in an ecosystem that provided me with equal opportunities for education, a job, and ultimately, the foundation to start my own business.

Looking back at my roots in Danta, a small village in Rajasthan, I see clearly how this ecosystem took shape. My father was a visionary, someone who understood that education was the only way to rise above the limitations of the lower middle class. He was a textile trader living in Kolkata, while the rest of us stayed in Danta. But he made sure we never felt the distance. It is from him that I learnt the value of education and community.

Danta was a village of just fifteen thousand people when I was growing up. But unlike many rural areas in India, Danta had schools that were fully equipped with standard infrastructure and all the essential amenities you would expect in a city school. We had sports fields, medical facilities, and *dharmsalas* (community centres), all thanks to the collective efforts of the people who came from this village and later succeeded in business. These successful families did not forget where they came from; they invested back into their village to ensure that future generations had the opportunities they never had.

Even the tradition of *chaanda* (collective contributions) played a key role in building much of the village's social infrastructure. It is this very spirit that helped create a culture of giving – a culture that made Danta what it is today.

The word *Bhamashah* comes to mind here – named after a minister who, during the reign of Maharana Pratap, donated all his wealth to support the Rajput warriors' army against Mughal invaders. This term has become synonymous with the selfless contribution in the Marwari community, where both time and money are given to build something larger than oneself. It is this deeply embedded principle of inclusive community participation that I witnessed growing up and one that continues to shape my worldview.

Thanks to this community ethos, both my primary and secondary schools were built by philanthropists and then handed over to the government to run. I also cannot leave out the teachers who nurtured us like family – they made sure we did not just learn from textbooks but from life itself.

After high school, I moved to Kolkata for higher studies. The city was overwhelming at first – where would I stay, what would I eat, and how would I make ends meet? Looking back, I realise how much these seemingly small questions shaped my journey. And it was in this very city that I again saw the power of community.

This is how each of my questions was addressed:

Where I stayed: Burrabazar was the heart of Kolkata's Marwari business community. During the day, people did business sitting on a *gaddi* – a mattress with a white cover. And at night, the same *gaddis* would be used for sleeping. It was common for students like me to be given a place to stay on these *gaddis*, often for little or no rent, all through the references of family members. Eventually, the Marwari community established two hostels – Poddar Chhatra Niwas and Halwasiya Chhatra Niwas – where students could stay for a nominal fee.

Where did I eat: Every building in Burrabazar had small family-run kitchens, providing home-cooked food at reasonable prices, called *basa.* I remember a man named Maharaj *ji,* who ran one of these kitchens. When I fell sick, he personally delivered meals to me, taking care of me like I was part of his own family. His kindness did not stop there – whenever someone was about to set off on a journey, he would always make sure to pack food for them. The prices were extremely affordable, and this ecosystem ensured that no one went hungry.

Later, I experienced the same sense of community in both Poddar Chhatra Niwas and Halwasiya Chhatra Niwas, where the mess facilities with collective kitchens provided affordable meals to students.

Where did I study: As I mentioned earlier, business was conducted in the *gaddis* during the day. This left little room for studying. That is when the Burrabazar Library came into being – an air-conditioned hall with an extensive collection of books and a peaceful place to study. The fee was incredibly low, and it became the perfect place for students like me to focus without distraction.

How did I make ends meet: Many students, including myself, took on part-time jobs to cover living expenses. I came from a Hindi-medium school and was a trained typist, so when an advertisement for a Hindi typist appeared in the newspaper, I took the opportunity. My father had always told me that while he would support my education, I was responsible for covering my own expenses. That simple skill of typing led to my first real job in the city.

This ecosystem, built on the foundations of inclusivity and mutual support, helped produce thousands of professionals, from chartered accountants to company secretaries, many of whom are now in influential positions around the world.

I hope that by reading this book, you will understand the immense power of an inclusive community and how small actions, when nurtured over time, can create a lasting impact.

The proverbs within are also a reflection of my own journey. I share them with the hope that the insights that have inspired me will also inspire you.

Sincerely,

B.L. Mittal

Index of Chapters

Chapter 1

Ram Ram sa

(राम राम सा)

* * *

*A timeless greeting for building trust in
business relations*

Have You Ever Heard a Greeting that Goes Beyond Mere Words?

The simple yet mighty Marwari salutation, *Ram Ram*, carries within itself a rich history and an even richer philosophy. Did you know it can be a powerful way to initiate business interactions? Let's explore.

A Welcoming Tradition

In the Marwari community, we treat our guests with the utmost respect. We see them as the embodiment of Lord Ram Himself. So when we say *Ram Ram*, we acknowledge this divine spark within each person.

You might wonder: does this greeting work for business meetings, too? Well, most Marwari business meetings begin with an exchange of *Ram Ram* and *Ram Ram sa*.

But when did this practice become a tradition? Well, it has been around for ages. The essence of business runs in the DNA of the Marwari community, and when a community excels in a particular field, that expertise becomes an integral part of its culture. It then gets passed down through generations in its colloquialisms, songs, and proverbs. The simple act of saying *Ram Ram* and *Ram Ram sa* exemplifies this tradition.

A Shared Vow

The impact of this greeting draws power from its profound philosophy. When the first speaker opens with *Ram Ram*, he not only offers a warm salutation but also subtly reveals himself as a devotee of the righteous Lord Ram. This expression of honesty becomes a silent promise – a vow to conduct business with the same integrity and commitment to duty that embodied the Lord Himself. *Ram Ram* then unfolds into a harmonious chord, composed of three beautiful notes:

1. *Pran jaye par vachan na jaye*, meaning I might lose my life, but I will never dishonour my word.

2. I adhere to a sattvic diet, nourishing myself with pure food. I believe all life forms are blessings of the Lord, and I intend them no harm.

3. I am my business partners' equal. I am capable of sitting across from them and taking our fraternity further.

The response of *Ram Ram sa* from the second businessperson echoes this sentiment. By uttering these words, they also position themselves as a *Ram ka banda* (the disciple of Shri Ram). Like their business partner, they too, promise to uphold their responsibilities with dignity and fairness, in line with their shared culture. The exchange of *Ram Ram* and *Ram Ram sa*, hence, translates into an oath of genuineness.

A Window into My Experiences

'Being Genuine' is my core value. It builds trust, the cornerstone of any successful business relationship. No matter the products you offer, the services you render, or the brand recognition that you have built, if trust is absent, your efforts amount to nothing. That's why I begin meetings with my fellow Marwaris with a warm and sincere *Ram Ram*. This greeting accomplishes three things in one go. First, it greets the other person. Second, it embodies my core values of authenticity, sattvic nourishment, and equal partnership. Third, it makes the fellow Marwari comfortable right at the beginning of the conversation.

When engaging with people outside the Marwari community, I adjust my approach to make it more culturally relevant. Here's how I introduce myself in business settings:

"Hello, my name is B.L. Mittal. I'm the Founder & Executive Chairman of SastaSundar. My organisation is a reflection of my core values and beliefs. And that's why 'Being Genuine' lies at the heart of SastaSundar.

We provide affordable, high-quality healthcare in a sustainable manner, and we partner with local communities through our Healthbuddy model. In fact, my core values are embodied in the very name of the organisation: 'Sasta' means economical and 'Sundar' stands for quality.

Similarly, we bring the words 'Health' and 'Buddy' together to address our local business partners. The name 'Healthbuddy' itself is a value-driven message for our customers. It speaks of their friendly, interpersonal connection with their local healthcare buddies.

And finally, our company culture is rooted in 'Being Child', because our childlike innocence and curiosity drive us to excellence – every day."

Now it's Your Turn!

In the world of business, nothing beats a good first impression. Would it not be powerful to greet your stakeholders with a gesture that fosters trust and respect? For your Marwari business partners or clients, consider opening your meetings with *Ram Ram*. This simple act of cultural appreciation will create a space for genuine conversation and connection.

Interacting with Diverse Cultures

While *Ram Ram* beats in the heart of the Marwari community, the underlying principle of establishing a psychological connection and trust is universal. Adapt your greetings to the other party's culture. For example, with English-speaking individuals, a warm 'Hello' or 'Good day' can be a good starting point. However, such greetings alone can sound quite generic. They lack the inherent gravity and depth of *Ram Ram*. In such cases, focus more on your core values in your introduction.

Here are three actionable steps to make your introductions stand out:

1. **Spotlight your company values:** Identify the practices that fuel your organisation and touch upon them in your introduction. True connection comes from authenticity, so ensure that your core values are principles that you actively practise. Here are a few examples to inspire you:

Inspiration 1: Technology Company (With a Focus on Green Energy)

"Good day, it is my pleasure to meet you! Our company is at the forefront of developing clean, renewable energy solutions. We are committed to reducing our carbon footprint and creating a sustainable future. Our products are designed to minimise environmental impact while maximising efficiency."

Inspiration 2: Food Production Company

"Hello, I'm delighted to introduce our company. We believe in nourishing both people and the planet. Our company is dedicated to organic farming practices, reducing food waste, and supporting local communities. We strive to provide healthy, delicious food without compromising our environmental responsibility."

Inspiration 3: Fashion Brand

"A very good day to you! Our brand is built on ethical fashion and sustainable practices. We use eco-friendly materials, support fair labour conditions, and minimise our industry's impact on the environment. Our goal is to create stylish clothing without sacrificing the planet."

A nuanced introduction can have far-reaching benefits. By transparently communicating the values embodied in your products, you lay the groundwork for justifying their prices in the future. This makes room for smoother and more straightforward negotiations.

2. **Keep the introduction direct and short:** Discuss your values and culture and any other salient features that define you and your organisation. However, avoid overloading the introduction with details, as this can dilute the greater purpose of the meeting. A concise introduction paves the way for a more conducive meeting.

3. **Present your values first, agenda later:** By presenting your core values upfront, you set the stage for a productive and positive meeting. This shows your commitment to integrity and purpose, fostering a more engaged and receptive audience.

So next time you step into a meeting room – whether virtual or face-to-face – bring along these principles because they tend to create lasting impressions almost effortlessly.

***

Chapter 2

Hathi taka ko

(हाथी टका को)

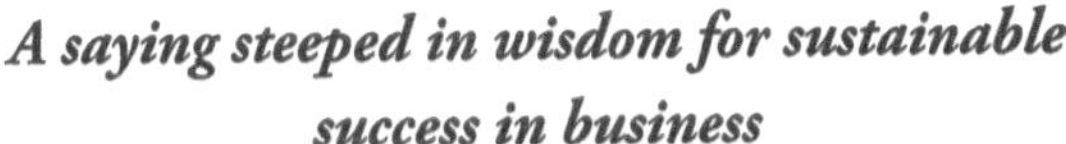

A saying steeped in wisdom for sustainable success in business

Would You Buy an Elephant for One Rupee?

Once upon a time, a smart and savvy Marwari businessman ran a cosy shop nestled in the town's big marketplace. He had a *munim* to help with his day-to-day dealings. One day, the accountant went out to run some routine errands. An unexpected sight met his eyes – a majestic elephant was up for sale in the market. Its skin shone like polished ebony, and its tusks reminded the *munim* of a pair of ivory sentinels. And the price tag? A mere rupee!

"One rupee?!" The shop owner, whom the *munim* called *Seth ji,* raised a sceptical eyebrow when he heard about the unbelievable opportunity. "But there must be some catch," he muttered under his breath. The wheels of his business acumen were turning rather quickly. "Surely, the animal must be sick," he declared finally. But the *munim* insisted, "No, *Seth ji*! This elephant looks as radiant as Lord Ganesh Himself. Such a divine symbol of prosperity!"

Drawn by curiosity and a lot of doubt, *Seth ji* and his *munim* took off to examine the marvel for themselves. And there it stood, the elephant, a towering symbol of strength and beauty – available for the astonishing price of one rupee. But instead of striking an immediate deal, the seasoned businessman paused. His mind calculated in silence. And after a moment of deliberation, he turned away, leaving the elephant behind – much to the *munim's* bewilderment.

The Lesson Revealed

Back at the shop, the *munim* could not hide his disappointment. "But *Seth ji,* why didn't we buy the elephant? It was practically free!"

A wise and knowing smile spread across *Seth ji's* face. "My dear *munim ji,*" he said, "you still have a lot to learn about the nuances of business. While the elephant itself might have been cheap, the cost of its upkeep – the mountains of food it would require – would amount to a staggering five hundred rupees a day. *Hathi taka ko, Munim ji* (The elephant eats money, my dear accountant)."

Beyond the Tale

The story is simple but comes with a thought-provoking lesson. Business success does not lie in flashy purchases or empty displays of wealth. It lies in acquiring only what truly fuels your enterprise. Cash flow, the lifeblood of any business, thrives on strategic operational decisions. So, every asset you invest in should be an asset that contributes to your bottom line. That way, your income will always exceed your expenditure, and this will ensure a healthy flow of operating cash.

A Window into My Experiences

In all my business decisions, I have consistently adhered to the principles exemplified in the above story. I have seen many of our competitors raise enormous amounts of capital and pursue costly acquisitions, only to fall into debt traps later on. Their temporary moments of glory quickly faded as they struggled with the burden of massive interest payments.

In contrast, at SastaSundar, we always focus on cost minimisation and avoid acquisitions that could lead to significant financial liabilities. This approach has positioned us as one of the most efficient organisations in our category. Our disciplined financial strategy has not only ensured long-term sustainability but also empowered us to build a resilient and purpose-driven organisation.

Now it's Your Turn!

Having heard the story of the elephant and the wise Marwari businessman and gained insight into my experience, think about how it applies to your own venture. Make sure your purchases are well-considered and contribute to long-term financial stability.

Take 10 minutes to audit your recent business purchases:

Step 1 (list your purchases): Jot down all the recent purchases you have made for your business.

Step 2 (ask yourself, "*Hathi taka ko?*"): For each purchase, assess the long-term impact on your cash flow. Will it generate enough revenue to offset its cost?

***

Chapter 3

Teebra mein paani, nav lakha lairr maani

(टीबड़ा में पानी, नव लखा लेर मानी)

A pearl of wisdom to weather any storm in your business

A Tale of a Diamond-studded Merchant

There once lived a wealthy merchant with a diamond necklace worth an astounding nine lakh rupees (*nav lakha haar* in Marwari literally means a necklace worth nine lakh rupees – which is roughly equal to nine crore rupees today). He was so proud of the beautiful piece of jewellery that he never took it off. The necklace was always seen adorning the merchant's chest.

One day, the merchant had to travel through a vast, perilous desert for an important business venture. As the scorching sun beat down mercilessly, the merchant's water supply reduced rapidly. Soon, he found himself thirsty and desperate. His throat started burning like a furnace, and his vision started blurring.

However, just as the merchant was about to give up all hope, he saw a shimmering mirage in the distance. No, it was not a cruel trick of the desert wind; it was a young woman carrying a precious pot of water fetched from a distant lake. Hope returned to the merchant's heart. He called out in a raspy voice, "*Beti*, let me have just one sip of water from your pot. God will bless you!"

The woman, wise beyond her years, paused to study the glittering necklace dangling from the merchant's neck. A slow smile played on her lips. "Of course, *kaka*," she replied, offering the life-giving water. "But you must bless me with that *nav lakha haar* of yours."

The merchant, tired and desperate, had little choice. He handed over his prized possession for a belly full of cool water – his temporary solace for a far greater loss.

Teebra mein paani, nav lakha lairr maani – a little water in the desert is a necklace worth a million dollars.

What Do We Learn

In the desert of the business world, liquidity is your precious pot of water. Despite the grand scale of your operations, the value of your inventory or the potential of your brand, you should always have a sufficient amount of readily available cash that you can feed back into your business. It is your safety net to catch you when you fall. It is your fuel to keep your engine running when the roads are rough and bumpy. Without it, even the most minor need (say, an unexpected expense or a sudden dip in sales) can force you to surrender your most valuable assets – sometimes at the price of peanuts.

However, remember that your profit is not the same as your cash flow from operations. Always plan to generate cash from your operations within a set timeframe. Profit without cash flow from operations is an illusion. Despite apparent profitability, it can only lead to severe cash crunches.

Moreover, do not confuse liquidity with your existing assets. A business may own a billion-dollar asset, but the same business can go bankrupt for the lack of a million dollars in liquidity.

A Window into My Experiences

While building SastaSundar, we saw many contemporary startups facing the harsh reality of having to sell their businesses or dilute their equity at undervalued prices. Unlike them, we have always managed to preserve our business integrity and retain full control of our equity. How was this possible? Well, this can be attributed to our unwavering focus on operational efficiency and maintaining a robust liquid war chest. By consciously avoiding liquidity traps, we ensured that we were never forced to make any desperate financial decisions. Our strategic approach helped us navigate the competitive landscape confidently, securing our position as a leader in the industry.

Now it's Your Turn!

Here are three actionable steps that you can take right away:

1. **Assess your current cash flow**: Track your income and expenses to understand your liquidity situation.

2. **Develop a liquidity plan:** Set a target for your cash reserves and create a plan to reach it. Look for ways to improve your cash flow – can you collect outstanding debts faster? Can you offer discounts for upfront payments? Remember – every little bit adds up.

3. **Explore options to improve your liquidity:** This could involve negotiating payment terms with suppliers, diversifying income streams, reducing unnecessary expenses, and so much more. The possibilities are endless!

***

Chapter 4

Ek punji, zameen do baar, teen guni, yash dischaar

(एक पुंजी, ज़मीन दो बार, तीन गुणी, यश दिसचार)

---✦---

The four essential pillars of a successful startup

One Saying, Fourfold Wisdom

Building a business from scratch is like navigating a maze with countless decisions at every turn. You need to formulate a clear value proposition, meticulously define your target audience, secure the right resources, and so much more. The to-do list is never-ending, and if not addressed correctly, it can quickly become overwhelming. So, where does one begin?

The Marwari business acumen offers valuable guidance. The proverb '*Ek punji, zameen do baar, teen guni, yash dischaar*' can be your strategic compass. Let's understand its profound philosophy.

Ek punji – be precise with capital

The Marwaris refer to capital as *punji*. The first element of the proverb, *ek punji*, suggests that the amount of capital you invest in launching your venture should be precisely what your business needs – not a penny more or less.

If you undercapitalise, you will face liquidity shortages that can hinder your growth and operations. But if you overcapitalise, you will tie up funds that could be more effectively utilised elsewhere. Plus, it will obligate you to pay unnecessary interest.

Zameen do baar – double down on infrastructure

Zameen in Hindi means land, and in the broader sense of the term, your overall infrastructure. The second element of the proverb, *zameen do baar*, speaks to the importance of overprovisioning infrastructure. In your business plan, always factor in twice as much infrastructure as is needed.

The logic is straightforward: success lies where opportunity meets preparation. You invest significant effort in launching your business, but without the necessary infrastructure, you will struggle to accommodate future growth. Today, you may start with a small plot of land to house all your machinery and staff. But tomorrow, your business might expand. Where will you then set up your new factory? Where will your newly hired team be based? Will any adjacent land be readily available?

To future-proof your business, make space for twice the required amount of land and infrastructure in your plan. By investing time in strategic planning now, you can avoid the costly delays associated with infrastructure development later.

Teen guni – triple down on talent and technology

Guni (meaning the talented one in Hindi) stands for a combination of cutting-edge technology and top-class human intelligence. The third element of our proverb, *teen guni*, focuses on these intellectual assets. You should always plan to onboard three times the amount of such resources that you need.

The reasoning is simple. In an ideal world, you will find talented team players right from the start, and they will continue contributing over the years as your business grows. However, in reality, employee turnover, market fluctuations, and talent scarcity are common challenges. Likewise, overprovisioning technology will make room for scalability, innovation, and the ability to quickly adapt to any unforeseen challenges or opportunities.

Yash dischaar – boost the signal for your brand

Yash in Marwari translates to goodwill and brand value. The final element of the proverb, *yash dischaar*, suggests planning a 360-degree promotion of your business (*dischaar* meaning all four directions). Seize every opportunity to market your business in a cohesive and consistent manner, exploring both traditional and digital media. Empower yourself and your team to adapt to emerging marketing techniques. Get noticed, stay relevant, and ensure that your brand leaves a lasting impression.

A Window into My Experiences

SastaSundar has always stood out in its category for raising the least amount of *punji* while avoiding the common practice of burning cash to boost GMV (gross merchandise volume). In contrast, our competitors, who secured substantial funding from investors, often ended up mismanaging their capital. Their entire ecosystems became heavily reliant on capital influxes. As a result, when the overarching capital regime became challenging for cash-burn models, their businesses took a hit. At SastaSundar, we have always treated capital with the utmost respect. It is our capital management policies that have positioned us as one of the most efficient organisations in our category.

Our digital-first strategy prioritises rapid brand expansion and scalability across multiple technological platforms. In today's age, therefore, *yash dischaar* is relatively easier for us to achieve. However, the principle of *teen guni* demands continuous effort and refinement. Global tech titans like Nvidia, Microsoft, and Google, alongside Indian counterparts like TCS and Infosys, have demonstrated the immense value derived from scaling technology and nurturing talented individuals.

Now it's Your Turn!

If you want to turn the proverb into practice, consider these actionable steps:

For *ek punji*

1. While formulating your business plan, make sure that the ecosystem you plan to build is not solely dependent on capital. Capital should just be one of the essential elements that bring your business model together. To draw a parallel with the human body, think of capital not as the heart of your anatomy but as the blood.

2. Hence, your focus should be on building the heart of your business first, like your core value proposition and operational strategy. Once this foundation is strong, focus on generating consistent cash flow. This will ensure the adequacy of capital, helping you meet financial obligations and return value to your investors without relying solely on continuous external funding.

For *zameen do baar*

1. Strike a balance between the availability of capital and your infrastructure planning. Our proverb suggests buying twice the amount of infrastructure you need. However, investing in additional land today does not mean that you are wasting your capital on unproductive assets. When expanding your business in the future, you might need additional adjacent land to build infrastructure commensurate with that growth.

   I have seen that many Marwari businesspeople take a long-term approach when setting up factories by investing in land and developing it in phases. This approach ensures that they are prepared for expansion without tying up too much capital upfront.

Please note that this may be less relevant for today's tech-based startups. Many of them prioritise flexibility and scalability over long-term asset ownership. By opting to rent larger properties from the outset, these companies can quickly adapt to changing business needs without the financial burden or time commitment associated with infrastructure development.

For *teen guni*

1. Technology is evolving at breakneck speed. Our proverb is relevant in today's world as it helps you mitigate the associated risks. The principle of *teen guni* suggests a proactive approach to technological change rather than a reactive one. Continuously research and adapt, ensuring your business is prepared to accommodate multiple technological changes.

2. Build progressive human resource practices and an enticing employer brand to attract top talent. Social media platforms like LinkedIn and Twitter are great for spotlighting your company culture and career opportunities to potential recruits.

For *yash dischaar*

1. *Yash* encompasses more than just building goodwill and a reputed brand. The proverb teaches us that the people in the state where you operate must first grasp and appreciate your company's core values. As you grow, this circle of understanding should expand in all directions, achieving a full 360-degree reach.

2. In today's world, with a strong digital presence and effective use of social media, you can reach a vast audience. While your

headquarters may be in one city or your factory in one state, your market spans the globe. Communicate your brand's goodwill and value to a global audience. Start by focusing on a small group and gradually extend your reach step by step.

***

Chapter 5

Ghaar ki jutti bhi saputi

(घर की जूती भी सपूति)

———✶✶———

A proverb about building emotional
connections in business

Would You Ever Fight Your Brother in Business?

Once upon a time, there were two brothers. They lived happily together, along with their wives and children, in the same house. However, one day, trouble found its way into paradise. The idyllic life of the brothers was disrupted by an issue as old as time – property. As the days passed, their minor disagreement escalated into a bitter feud. Finally, in an effort to resolve the dispute, they took the matter to court. But they ended up spending hours hurling blame at each other. Neither the legal counsel nor the judge was able to call a truce.

Exhausted after a long day in court, the younger brother left the courtroom to head home. Right outside, his gaze fell upon his elder brother's shoes, neatly placed in one corner. They were beautiful leather shoes with exquisite craftsmanship. Concerned about the potential damage, he turned to his son, who was accompanying him. "*Beta,*" he instructed, "protect your *tau ji's* shoes from the harsh sunlight. Move them into the shade."

The older brother, who was coming out of the courtroom at the moment, overheard his brother. Guilt and remorse washed over him. He realised the absurdity of their conflict. He thought, "Who am I fighting? My own blood, my own brother! The person I grew up with, the person with whom I share a household. He is attentive to even my shoes, and I'm treating him so poorly." Overwhelmed, he went up to his younger brother and extended an apology. "I'm sorry, *bhai,*" he said. "I have made a terrible mistake. Let us sit down and resolve the issue." The younger brother, equally emotional, accepted the olive branch.

The discussion that followed achieved what hours of legal proceedings could not – a mutual understanding. The elder brother, humbled by his brother's kindness, recognised his sibling's superior worldly wisdom. With newfound respect, he willingly handed over the entire property.

Ghaar ki jutti bhi saputi – the household shoe is as good as a well-mannered daughter. Familiar things, even if ordinary, hold immense value.

What Do We Learn

In Marwari business households, you often see brothers and family members running ventures together as a single unit. How do they do this with so much aplomb? They leave no room for misunderstandings in their business decision-making. Strong, harmonious relationships form the foundation of their venture. This is true even if your business partner is not a family member. All stable business foundations are built on strong partnerships and mutual trust.

In the above story, the younger brother's care for his elder brother's belongings exemplifies the importance of respect and empathy in business relationships. Understanding and valuing each other's contributions are essential for long-term success.

Equally important is effective communication. Addressing issues promptly and openly helps maintain trust and prevents conflicts from escalating.

Finally, the elder brother's decision to entrust the property to his younger brother sheds light on the importance of having long-term foresight. Focusing on the overall success of the business rather than short-term gains is important for sustainable growth.

A Window into My Experiences

At SastaSundar, our culture is rooted in the concept of 'Being Child', which cultivates a strong emotional connection across the organisation. This bond has been instrumental in building the company and maintaining a cohesive team over time.

A wonderful example is Taniya Roy, a bright girl who worked with me at SastaSundar and later relocated to Australia for personal reasons. Despite the move, she continues to stay connected and has contributed wholeheartedly to this book project, going above and beyond any commercial consideration. Her dedication exemplifies the spirit of *saputi* and demonstrates the power of emotional connection.

Now it's Your Turn!

Emotional connection is a powerful business asset. While operating a business with your brother (or a family relative) is not necessary, treating your co-founder like a brother is mandatory. Extend these feelings of trust and understanding to your wider team as well. The day you start considering each employee as a family member, you will start watching the magic unfold.

Human relations in HR practices cannot be governed by standard operating procedures or rulebooks; they flourish through shared values. Make this the very essence of your organisational culture.

Three pillars support such a culture:

1. **Clarity of purpose:** Every team member should understand the company's mission, vision, and goals. This shared understanding provides a sense of direction and unity.

2. **Value-driven practices:** All policies and procedures should align with your core values. This ensures that all the actions you take are consistent with the organisational beliefs and commitments.

3. **Communication and responsiveness**: Open dialogue is essential for building trust and strong relationships. This includes active listening, shared decision-making, and creating a platform for everyone's voice to be heard.

*****

Chapter 6

Kamar jhuki loto liyo, nadi det bhandaar, je haadha mein akdan hui, saath let bhabtaar

(कमर झुकी, लोटो लियो, नदी देत भंडार, जे हाडा में अकड़न हुई, साथ लेत भवतार)

❖

A wise saying about the importance of humility and respect in business

A Divine Approach to Seeking Wisdom

I would like to start this chapter with a great example from the life of Lord Ram. Despite defeating Ravan in battle, Ram held immense respect for the demon king and his worldly wisdom.

After the battle, when Ravan lay mortally wounded on the ground, Ram instructed his brother Lakshman to approach Ravan and seek his knowledge of life. But Lakshman returned empty-handed, explaining that Ravan had refused to share any wisdom.

Ram asked his brother, "Dear Lakshman, where were you standing while making this request?" "I stood near Ravan's head," Lakshman replied, "But how does that relate to Ravan's refusal to share any wisdom with us?" He was confused.

A knowing smile graced Lord Ram's face. He explained, "Brother, when seeking something from another, one should approach their feet, not their head."

I believe this piece from mythology perfectly captures the meaning of the Marwari proverb that we are about to explore.

The Science Behind the Saying

Imagine a fast-flowing river. If you want to draw water from it using a *lota*, you have to bend down and collect it carefully with precision. But if you want to draw the water while standing tall, the height will obscure the water's surface. This could cause you to slip and fall in. Even worse, the river's powerful current might sweep you away.

The Power of Humility in Business

The analogy above demonstrates our proverb's depth and practical significance. It has a wonderful lesson to teach: ego has no place in the world of entrepreneurship.

Just as the individuals who bend to drink from the river are rewarded with sustenance, businesses that approach the market with humility and respect are more likely to thrive. *Kamar jhuki loto liyo, nadi det bhandaar.*

Conversely, arrogance can lead to downfall, much like a person being swept away by the river's current. *Je haadha mein akdan hui, saath let bhabtaar.*

A Window into My Experiences

In both my personal life and the businesses I have built with my team, I have always made politeness a top priority. We have seen firsthand how countless conflicts, which could have escalated into bitter feuds, were resolved through polite dialogue.

Our business journey has its share of mistakes and unmet customer demands. However, we have learnt that acknowledging failures and rectifying them with politeness works wonders.

We encapsulated this philosophy in one of Microsec's campaigns as well. The tagline went like –

I listen to Microsec because Microsec listens to me.

This simple message reflected our commitment to active listening and a customer-centric approach. By following it, we have been able to build strong relationships with our customers and create a positive brand image.

Now it's Your Turn!

Humility is not about self-deprecation; it is about recognising that you are part of a larger ecosystem. Consider these practical steps:

1. **Listen to the market:** The business market is a deceptive space. In its competitive environment, it is easy for leaders to become intoxicated by success. However, it is precisely in these moments that humility can become your most potent weapon. A humble leader is more receptive to market feedback because, on the flip side of success, there are setbacks. Your humility and open-mindedness determine how you respond to challenges and whether you overcome them.

2. **Stay grounded:** Avoid the arrogance that can lead to complacency. Remain vigilant and seek ways to improve your offerings and serve your customers better. By being open to constructive criticism, you stay quick on your feet when responding to changing market dynamics.

3. **Build stronger relationships :** Invest time in building rapport with your business partners and suppliers. When you approach them with humility, you are seen as approachable and open to dialogue. This can lead to valuable partnerships, reduced conflicts, and a stronger market position.

4. **Encourage innovation:** Innovation is not a department; it is a mindset. A culture of humility encourages open communication, risk-taking, and experimentation. For this specific reason, we named SastaSundar's office 'Innovation Tower' and our facility 'Elevation Centre' rather than a traditional 'Fulfilment Centre'. These names symbolised our aspiration to elevate our team's thinking and inspire them to reach new heights.

***

Chapter 7

Moongphaali se aave bandra, sono diya log, bhagdari se bhaagya khule, daan diya paarlok

(मूंगफली से आवे बांदरा, सोनो दिया लोग, भागदारी से भाग्य खुले, दान् दिया परलोक)

The four essential elements of a people-centric business

A Sermon by Lord Krishna

You are all familiar with the great Lord Krishna and his devoted friend, Sudama. Despite Krishna's status as a king and Sudama's life as a poor Brahmin, their bond was strong. One day, Sudama brought Krishna a modest gift of three bowls of rice.

Deeply touched by this gesture, Krishna decided to reciprocate. He was the ruler of the three *loks* or *tri-lok (Satyalok, Bhulok and Paatal lok* or the kingdoms of Heaven, Earth, and Netherworld). Krishna bestowed one of these kingdoms on Sudama. As you can imagine, each of the *loks* was priceless. In today's terms, they would surpass a billion dollars.

Krishna's wife, Rukmini, was astonished by her husband's decision. She questioned his generosity, "*Nath*, what are you doing? I feel such a grand gift is excessive. Do you intend to gift all three *loks* to Sudama for the three bowls of rice?" Hearing this, Krishna gently replied, "*Priya* Rukmini, this exchange is beyond giving three kingdoms in return for three bowls of rice. Those three bowls of rice were all that Sudama had. By that token, I should have given him all that I have. By offering him a kingdom, I only attempted to restore some balance."

One Simple Saying, Four Profound Truths

Likewise, in the contemporary corporate world, your people are the heartbeat of your business. You should always value their contributions and reciprocate in equal measure. A well-known Marwari *lokokti* captures this philosophy quite well. With Lord Krishna's blessings, let's explore the proverb piece by piece.

Part I: Peanuts Attract None but the Apes

Moongphaali se aave bandra. The first piece of our proverb is obvious: just as *moongphaali* (peanuts) lure *bandra* (monkeys), low compensation only attracts mediocre talent. To build a formidable team, you need to offer more than just basic salaries. Quality talent seeks work environments where their contributions are recognised and rewarded. You must offer competitive pay and benefits to attract individuals who can drive your business forward.

Part II: Gold Attracts Gold

Sono diya log. The second piece also delivers a straightforward message: if you want to have a *sone ki* team that is a golden team, you must pay for it. To attract and retain the best talent in your organisation, you must be willing to invest significantly in them in the form of competitive salaries. Quality compensation packages signal to employees that their skills and efforts are valued. This investment builds loyalty encourages higher productivity and attracts top-tier talent who can help scale your business effectively.

Part III: Partnerships are Your Growth Engine

Bhagdari se bhaagya khule. The third part is equally profound: partnerships are powerful catalysts for growth. By bringing on a business partner, you can not only gain new perspectives but also get access to additional resources and have someone to share your responsibilities with. When done strategically, business partnerships can open doors to new markets, technologies and even customer bases. Your business becomes better at navigating challenges and seizing opportunities that you might not have been able to tackle alone.

The concept of partnership is actually expansive. It starts with your co-founding team with whom you share ownership and extends to your employees with whom you share ESOPs (employee stock ownership plans), and from there on to your investors, your customers, the government, and ultimately, society at large.

Part IV: The Ultimate Fulfilment is in Giving Back

Daan diya paarlok. The fourth and final piece of our puzzle sheds light on an eternal truth: if you want peace in life, give back to the community that has already given you so much.

Beyond personal satisfaction, corporate philanthropy boosts your company's reputation and builds goodwill. It reflects a commitment to social responsibility and ethical values that can resonate deeply with your customers and stakeholders. It can also cultivate a sense of higher purpose and fulfilment among your employees.

This philosophy of giving back is all the more relevant in today's era of climate change. Human beings have taken so much from nature. It is imperative that we adopt practices that restore and enrich the planet in our personal and professional lives.

A Window into My Experiences

The Marwaris embody this *lokokti* with great practicality. In their traditional joint family setups, wealth is divided equally among brothers. In nuclear setups, cousins look out for and care for each other.

I applied the same family principle to my businesses as well. When we were planning Microsecs' IPO (initial public offering), we established a trust holding 5% equity for our employees. Allocating shares to our team had a magical impact. Our retention rate rose to industry-leading levels as employees contributed wholeheartedly to the company. As we grew in our business, so did their personal success.

Moreover, my own journey – from schooling in a hostel to my children's education – reflects the kindness and support I have received from others. My current reality is a direct result of their generosity. I believe, that despite my efforts to give back, I can never fully repay my debt to society.

Now it's Your Turn!

A thriving business transcends financial performance; it focuses on creating a positive impact. Here are a few steps you can take to achieve this:

1. Align your team's contributions with KPIs (key performance indicators) and reward them for achieving these goals. Clearly define roles and expectations from the outset so that there is mutual understanding. Next, establish how you will measure the deliverables. These measurements will then become your KPIs. KPI-linked incentives always drive top performance.

2. ESOP is a wonderful tool for employee motivation. Global evidence suggests that well-structured ESOP policies can significantly boost team morale. But it is crucial to move beyond mere paperwork. The benefits of the ESOP should be tangible, and the goal should be achievable. And at the end of the term, liquidity must be ensured.

3. Learn from the legends to understand how co-founding teams and ESOPs are structured. Read up in detail on the

RHPs (red herring prospectuses) that are available on SEBI's website. Some of the RHPs you must refer to are those of DMart, Zomato, and Policy Bazaar, as well as the pioneering Infosys from the 1990s.

***

Chapter 8

Maang jathe, daam bathe

(माँग जठे, दाम बठे)

*A wise adage on the dynamic interplay between
demand and supply*

A Window into My Experiences

I would like to start this chapter with an anecdote from my
life. This proverb has been the north star of my entrepreneurial
journey. It was imparted to me by my father. He was a man of
many insights.

After graduating from college in Rajasthan, I came to Kolkata,
West Bengal, with aspirations of becoming a CA (chartered
accountant). When I had expressed this desire, my pragmatic
father had said, "*Beta*, pursue what your heart desires. But I have
only one condition: you must earn your way through it. I can

fund your studies, but I want you to experience the satisfaction of achieving your goals through hard work."

And so it had begun. However, as a CA articleship trainee at that time, I was earning a modest stipend of three hundred rupees a month. Meanwhile, my monthly expenses were around thirty-two hundred rupees.

I researched and found out that the average monthly income of a qualified accountant was thirty-five hundred rupees. But with only six to seven hours to spare per week, I struggled to imagine how I would earn the remaining amount. I felt stuck, as I lacked the required skillset, and nobody was likely to pay me that much. But I was determined to earn my keep, as I had promised my father.

And ultimately, it was my father who once again showed me the path. One day, he handed me a Hindi newspaper that had an advertisement for a Hindi typist. I did not waste a minute applying for that job and was soon contacted for an interview. The newspaper needed someone to type letters in Hindi for its readership and business connections in Uttar Pradesh and Bihar.

When I arrived for the interview, I saw that I was the only applicant. I knew that I had to seize the opportunity. The managing director, after interviewing me, said, "Mittal, we're in dire need of your skills. Can you start tomorrow?"

My full-time studies and traineeship conflicted with this offer. I apologised, "Sorry, sir, I'm unable to start tomorrow. But I can commit to working a full six hours every Saturday," and then hesitantly added, "In return, I would request to be compensated with thirty-two hundred rupees per month, sir."

The managing director stood up and exclaimed in disbelief, "What are you saying? Who would pay you so much for only six hours of work per week!" Hearing this, I also calmly stood up from my chair and replied, "No problem, sir. I will leave."

Sensing that I might actually walk out and recognising the rarity of Hindi typists in Bengal, he regained his composure soon. The managing director invited me to sit down, have a cup of tea and reconsider. He was a practical man. "I agree with all your demands, Mittal," he said finally, "It's just that I need to send the Hindi letters daily. If I receive a letter from a merchant today, I need to type and send my reply by tomorrow."

I saw the problem as an opportunity to come up with an innovative solution. "Sir, how about you let me take a Hindi typewriter home? I will come to your office every evening and collect the letters from you. I will then complete the typing at night and drop them off in the morning. Does this arrangement work for you?"

Our agreement was prompt, and the arrangement we made ran smoothly for three long years with a continuous flow of work. It was a classic win-win outcome.

What Do We Learn

Even a small skill can have immense value. The key is to identify whether there is a demand in the market and to choose your work accordingly.

In my case, the scarcity of Hindi typists in West Bengal at the time played to my advantage. The few available typists were prohibitively expensive, which created a unique opportunity for me. By recognising this gap in the market, I was able to offer my services at a competitive rate and secure a steady stream of work.

If you want to thrive in the business world, always make sure that your demand (*maang*) in the market outstrips the overall supply. Your business idea does not need to be groundbreaking or revolutionary. Even a simple product or skill, if in demand, can catapult your business to remarkable heights.

Maang jathe, daam bathe – escalating demands inevitably lead to rising prices.

Now it's Your Turn!

My experiences have taught me that success lies in identifying the right market opportunities. Without a fundamental knowledge of where market demand is coming from, you might risk building castles in the sand.

So, always keep an eye out for untapped markets. Conduct rigorous research to pinpoint what people need but cannot get. Once you are able to identify the unmet demands, half of the battle is won. Proceed then to test your product-market fit through rapid prototyping and iterative customer feedback. After that, develop a clear value proposition that directly addresses the customers' pain points. Your product or service must solve a real problem.

Remember, big things come from small beginnings. So, never be afraid to start small. But remain vigilant – the market is a treacherous place, and it is ever-evolving. Continuously monitor the customers' behaviour and market trends. Agility and adaptability are paramount for your long-term success.

Your offering must be consistently unique to stand out.

***

Chapter 9

Khulya kiwad duniyadari, band kiwad Marwari

(खुल्या कीवाड़ दुनियादारी, बंद कीवाड़ मारवाड़ी)

A perfect reflection of the spirit of the global Marwaris

Would You Eat Fries with a Dip of *Rabri*?

I am a simple Marwari businessman. My work takes me across cities, countries, and even continents. I meet diverse people every day. I understand their thought processes and connect with them. I learn their languages, sit across from them, and establish business relationships. This is the nature of business, I believe.

Yet, we Marwaris possess a distinct identity. While we engage with the outer world, we never lose touch with our inherent roots. Our culture is deeply ingrained in us because, at the end of the day, it is in our DNA. So whether in a bustling metropolis or a quaint village, we carry our heritage with us. We might savour potato fries with tomato dip while travelling, but at home, it is *bajra ki roti* with *rabri ki* dip for us.

This is because when we go out, we become global citizens. We behave in worldly ways. We dress formally and indulge in global cuisine. But when we come home, we revert to our traditions. We become true-blue Marwaris. We apply *tilak* on our foreheads and sit together to enjoy our *roti* with *rabri*.

What Do We Learn

The Marwari community's progress can be attributed to its ability to seamlessly blend tradition with modernity. This delicate balance of identity has been our strength. Building bridges while preserving our core values is how we connect.

To thrive in today's interconnected world, you must be inclusive. Make every person you engage with feel welcomed and understood, regardless of their background. This harmonious coexistence, much like the seamless blend of milk and water, is the essence of the Marwari spirit. Make this your spirit, too.

A Window into My Experiences

At SastaSundar, we have always been careful about balancing a modern office culture with traditional values. This delicate balance is evident in our commitment to fostering a culture of innovation and experimentation, such as implementing agile methodologies and encouraging cross-functional collaboration, while simultaneously upholding the rich Indian traditions, like celebrating festivals with employee-led initiatives.

This approach has also influenced my interactions with clients. During my time at Microsec, I interacted with clients from diverse backgrounds. I observed that meetings with Bengali clients at the Bengal Club, Punjabi clients at the Punjab Club, and Marwari clients at the Bengal Rowing Club or Hindustan Club often yielded positive results. The meeting location was instrumental in each case. I have always aligned myself with my clients' cultural preferences. I believe negotiating on someone's home turf significantly increases your chances of success.

Now it's Your Turn!

Just as the Marwaris thrive in diverse environments, embrace diverse perspectives and markets. But be sure to maintain your core values at all times. Like the Marwaris emphasise family and community, uphold strong ethical principles and social responsibility.

The ability to blend tradition with modernity is just as important. You must be agile in adopting new technologies and market trends while preserving your core competencies. Look beyond traditional boundaries and seek opportunities that cater to a broader audience.

***

Chapter 10

Sonar hi sono batasi (सुनार है सोनो बतासी) and Bawla na ittar diya khajasi, aur keh si mitho hai

(बावला नं इत्तर दिया खाजासी, और कह सी मिठो है)

------ ❖ ------

Two practical perspectives on the criticality of expertise

Wisdom's Twin Pillars

In this chapter, I will focus on two *lokoktis*. Both are connected, but each is as insightful as the other. The central thought is simple: knowledge is power, but expert counsel is the compass.

Proverb I: The Goldsmith Knows Gold

Imagine you possess a gold coin, but you are unsure of its exact value. It is heavy, perhaps 5 grams, 10 grams, or somewhere in between. Its true worth is unclear. But to fully use it in the market, you must know its real value. Personal guesses, family opinions, or neighbourly advice might seem helpful – but unfortunately, none can provide definitive answers. The goldsmith, an expert, is the only one who can truly assess the coin's value. Hence the saying – *sonar hi sono batasi* – only the goldsmith can tell the worth of gold.

Parallel to this, in today's corporate environment, if you seek genuine insights into your field or industry trends, consult someone truly adept and knowledgeable.

Proverb II: The madman tastes the perfume as sweet

Now, the second *lokokti* – *bawla na ittar diya khajasi, aur keh si mitho hai.* If you offer perfume (*ittar*) to a *bawla* or a madman, he will not know whether to apply it or throw it away. He would end up eating it and declaring it sweet. The proverb highlights the absurdity of seeking advice from the unqualified.

Therefore, when it comes to business counsel, approach someone who possesses deep practical knowledge and expertise. Their insights can guide you in making informed decisions, rather than leading you down a misguided path.

A Deep Dive into the Dictums

The modern business world is evolving at an unprecedented pace. Your instinct is valuable, but it may be based on past experiences and may not fully align with the current challenges. It may even be influenced by personal biases or emotions. Relying solely on instinct can, therefore, increase your likelihood of making impulsive decisions that overlook potential consequences.

The solution is to seek a second opinion – turn to experts whom you can trust. Though well-meaning, friends and family may be emotionally invested in your success, leading to biased advice. So, when it comes to complex business decisions, consulting experts should be your go-to approach for a more objective perspective.

Here's what to look for in a mentor:

- **Specialised knowledge**: Choose someone with an in-depth understanding and experience in your specific business domain. They can offer insights, strategies, and solutions that are tailored to your unique challenges.

- **Awareness of industry trends**: A good mentor stays on top of industry trends – both ongoing and upcoming. They are conversant with domain regulations and best practices. They can help you spot opportunities and mitigate risks.

- **Brilliant problem-solving skills:** Experts excel at analysing complex problems and suggesting effective solutions. Their structured approach can be invaluable in decision-making.

- **Extensive network and resources:** A well-connected mentor can leverage their vast network and resources to support and grow your business.

A Window into My Experiences

My experiences founding Microsec and SastaSundar led me to categorise challenges into two areas. For issues within my and the team's expertise, we made independent decisions.

However, when knowledge gaps existed, we consistently sought advice from specialised experts. Contrary to the notion that high fees guarantee quality, I have observed that expensive consultants often provide defensive, structural recommendations rather than straightforward, practical solutions. At Microsec and SastaSundar, we have always prioritised vertical domain expertise for its direct and actionable insights.

Now it's Your Turn!

Our proverb duo strongly suggests that expertise lies at the core of business sustainability. Here are some actionable steps to strengthen your foundation:

1. When faced with complex decisions, seek a second opinion to gain a distinct, valuable perspective.

2. Choose a consultant with a proven track record. Thoroughly research potential advisers, focusing on their expertise and ethical standards.

3. Clearly define expected deliverables and costs with your consultant from the start to ensure mutual understanding.

At the end of the day, remember that you hold the final authority. While seeking advice is essential, there are certain critical decisions in your life that only you can make. No adviser can take the lead there.

Take inspiration from the Ramayana: even with numerous *gurus* and advisers, Lord Ram made all the ultimate choices that determined his outcome in the battle against Ravan.

***

Chapter 11

Kaano tu, main kyun dekhu tedho? Jadh gelo saaval pariya hai, kyun chaleya tedho medho?

(कांनौ तू, मैं क्यों देखू टेड़ो? जद गेलो सावल परिया है, क्यों चालय टेड़ो मेड़ो?)

——❖——

A proverb on the importance of having a positive outlook in business

My Tryst with Visionaries

Having collaborated with industry veterans and seasoned professionals for over thirty years now, I have learnt that they consistently emphasise one key principle. This principle embodies the essence of the proverb we are about to explore.

But first, a little anecdote.

A Window into My Experiences

I had the privilege of working closely with Shree Prahlad Rai *ji* Agarwala, the chairman of Rupa & Co., who is a truly savvy businessman. Agarwala *ji* has never made a single decision in his life that could be deemed negative.

I recall an instance when one of his biggest competitors acted against him with ill intent. Upon learning this, I suggested that he retaliate in equal measure. I remember him sitting me down and explaining, "Banwari, you see, thinking and acting negatively is the competitor's hallmark, not ours. He is simply doing what aligns with the values ingrained in his DNA. We, however, must adhere to the core values ingrained in ours." And true to his words, the decisions and consequent actions Agarwala *ji* took, even in the face of such a serious adversary, were remarkably positive.

Positivity is a Winner

In the playground of business, you need the perfect 20/20 vision. It helps you see (and think) clearly ahead and also reflect back with insight. A hasty, bad decision taken today might hit you hard tomorrow. Additionally, the choices you make now must be informed by the lessons learnt yesterday. You learn and grow as you go, and a positive attitude helps tie everything together.

But you are rarely the only player on the field. Imagine being paired with an opponent whose vision is distorted and perspective skewed. Does that mean that you should also adjust your view to match theirs? Well, if the road ahead is clear, why should you choose the winding detour? It is a common human tendency to respond in kind when treated unjustly. However, our proverb offers a clear guide for those with logical minds.

Kaano tu, main kyun dekhu tedho? Jadh gelo saaval pariya hai, kyun chaleya tedho medho?

It essentially addresses your opponent, saying, "Your vision is unclear *(kaano tu)*, why should I follow your distorted view (*main kyun dekhu tedho*)? When the path ahead is clear (*jadh gelo saaval pariya hai*), why should I walk crookedly (*kyun chaleya tedho medho*)?"

In your business endeavours, always prioritise positivity and a clear, direct approach.

Now it's Your Turn!

When external pressures become relentless, your internal fortitude must be even stronger. Here are a few steps that will help you:

1. **Practise ethical leadership:** Demonstrate integrity and honesty in all your business dealings. By doing so, you can cultivate a company culture where ethical behaviour is the standard. This will inspire trust and respect among your team and customers.

2. **Ignore external noise:** Focus on building your internal foundation. By tuning out distractions and competitors' negative tactics, you can focus on building strong customer relationships. It pays off in the long run, as you will have their unwavering support and loyalty even in the face of an adversary.

3. **Develop a long-term perspective:** Your decisions should be grounded in sustainability rather than short-term gains or reactive measures. By following this, you can establish a solid foundation that can respond to any market shifts.

4. **Build resilience:** Cultivate a steadfast mindset to weather any storm effectively. This means developing the capacity to bounce back from setbacks, maintaining a positive outlook, and focusing on finding solutions.

***

Chapter 12

Sono napu dus baraas, maati saal pachis, kaushal napu ee janam, parmarth janam battis

(सोनो नापु दस बरस, माटी साल पच्चीस, कौशल नापु ई ज़नम, परमार्थ ज़नम बत्तिस)

A proverb on thoughtful investments and the use of resources

At the End of the Day, What is the Purpose of the Money That We Earn?

Money is undeniably a powerful resource. It caters to our material needs, comforts, and much more. But when used wisely, it holds the potential to transform lives. Money can open doors to opportunities – allowing us to create, give back, and experience the world in new and meaningful ways. By making conscious decisions about how we earn, save, and spend, we can create a life full of purpose and abundance.

The proverb we are going to explore in this chapter reflects this idea. It is composed of four parts, each guiding us on how to utilise our hard-earned money wisely and effectively. Let's understand it piece by piece.

Part I: Gold Lasts a Decade

Sono napu dus baraas. The first piece of the proverb says, investing in *sono* or gold yields returns for a relatively short-term investment horizon. The underlying implication is the suitability of gold for specific investment styles. When you invest in gold, it starts yielding potential profit normally in a cycle of ten years. Its liquid nature means it can be easily bought and sold. So, gold is a viable option for you if you have a ten-year perspective.

Part II: Land Yields for a Quarter-Century

Maati saal pachis. The second part literally translates to: land for twenty-five years. Unlike gold, which offers returns within a decade, land investments generally require a longer-term outlook. Land is relatively less liquid, making it less suitable for quick sale. Therefore, it is a suitable investment over a twenty-five-year horizon. It is ideal for you if you have a patient investment strategy.

Part III: Skills Last a Lifetime

Kaushal napu ee janam. The third part is eternally essential: skill or *kaushal* is the dynamic engine propelling human progress. If you learn a skill and master its applications, it will take care of your livelihood throughout your life.

However, while skills are invaluable, they are still a finite resource within an individual's lifespan. Unlike renewable assets, skills can lose their edge without consistent nurturing. To maximise their potential, invest in lifelong learning. It is through the acquisition and refinement of new knowledge that you can extend the utility of your skills.

Part IV: Welfare Lasts Long Enough to Earn You Salvation

Parmarth janam battis. The final part of the proverb is symbolic in its representation of time. It suggests that actions rooted in selflessness and compassion (*parmarth*) have a long-lasting impact. By engaging in charitable deeds and social causes, you can accumulate positive *karma* or righteousness that extends beyond this life and into future existences – or symbolically speaking – into thirty-two lifetimes. This aligns with many spiritual and philosophical traditions that emphasise the importance of giving back to society.

The Intangible Edge

In today's knowledge economy, the intangible assets of a business often outweigh the tangible ones in value. Skillset accumulation lies at the heart of this shift. It is not merely about theoretical knowledge but the practical application of skills that truly drives success. This emphasis on human capital, rather than physical assets, is reshaping industries and economies.

Additionally, the concept of social empowerment has never been more relevant. As you develop new competencies, you gain the ability to contribute more meaningfully to your community and drive positive change. This is where the enduring nature of *dharma* aligns with a modern perspective.

A Window into My Experiences

I want to share a simple life experience here. My father was a diversified investor; he allocated some funds to real estate, some to land, a bit more to stocks and some to fixed deposits. But among all his investments, the most valuable one was in my education. This investment has proven to be the most rewarding. While his tangible assets like the house, land and stocks have been liquidated, the skills he nurtured in me continue to support my family.

My first venture was Microsec. While the company has evolved, the core team members' expertise and dedication remain intact as they now lead SastaSundar. In today's world, where intellectual capital and skill-based businesses are increasingly valued, their potential for sustained profitability and longevity is more evident than ever.

Now it's Your Turn!

In a world obsessed with short-term gains, resist the temptation of quick wins. Our proverb reminds us that true, sustainable growth is built on a strong foundation of skills and ethical practices.

Personal growth is a lifelong journey. Here are a few actionable steps you can take to get started:

1. **Cultivate a growth mindset:** View obstacles as opportunities for growth and learning. Stay curious and seek knowledge from diverse sources. Develop the ability to bounce back from setbacks.

2. **Prioritise self-care:** Maintain clear boundaries between your work and personal life. Regularly exercise, eat healthily, and sleep well for optimal performance. Incorporate mindfulness, meditation, or other stress management techniques.

On a similar note, engaging in social responsibility is not just about altruism; it is a strategic necessity. Here are my suggestions if you want to make a true difference:

1. **Practice environmental sustainability:** Adopt environmentally friendly practices within your business operations. Reduce waste generation through recycling and waste management programmes. Invest in energy-efficient technologies.

2. **Ensure ethical sourcing:** Ensure that your suppliers adhere to fair labour and environmental standards. Verify that your products are sourced responsibly and be transparent about sourcing practices and supply chain information.

3. **Support the local economy:** Expand your operations to create more job opportunities. Partner with local educational institutions for skill development programmes.

***

Chapter 13

Pehle likh, peeche de, bhul padhe toh kagaz se le

(पहले लिख, पीछे दे, भूल पड़े तो काग़ज़ से ले)

A proverb that highlights the importance of real-time accounting of transactions

Of Records and Business

The *lokokti* of this chapter is simple yet directional. It spotlights the value of proper record-keeping. Marwari practices in this area align with the *Mahajani khata paddhati*, a well-regarded and scientific accounting method that is recognised as one of the oldest forms of record-keeping.

Can You Recall Every Transaction from Yesterday?

Maybe, yes. But what about a particular transaction from last year? Or one from ten years ago? The sheer volume of business dealings might make that a daunting task. Marwari businesspeople understand that the seeds of tomorrow's success are sown today. So they plan in advance.

Pehle likh – write first – emphasises the need to record every transaction in your accounting books. A business is a dynamic web of countless conversations, interactions, and exchanges over time. Even the sharpest mind can falter in remembering every small business dealing.

Therefore, plan before taking action. Make a note of the transaction before it occurs.

The second step – *peeche de* – is to then proceed with the transaction.

Should your memory fail or *bhul padhe*, you can always *kagaz se le* or refer to your records to avoid errors or losses.

Own Your Accounting

In business, ignorance is not bliss. It is actually a financial drain, as actual losses often exceed accounting losses. You must have a firm grip on your own books.

Our proverb encourages a disciplined approach to business where every transaction is accounted for. By maintaining accurate records, you are able to establish trust with your business partners. You are also able to manage risks better – proper bookkeeping helps identify potential financial risks in advance. And last but not least, referring to past records can provide valuable insights for future decisions.

A Window into My Experiences

From a very young age, my father instilled in me the importance of meticulous record-keeping. Even when I was a student living in Rajasthan, he would send me monthly money orders with strict instructions to document every expense. This practice helped me reduce waste, avoid overspending, and cultivate the habit of saving.

However, with time, I came to realise that maintaining accounts is just one aspect of financial discipline. I have seen that my father kept all of his accounts, but his financial investments were not always prudent. He worked hard but often lent money that was never recovered. This made me realise that record-keeping and financial discipline are not the same.

My father's experience inspired me to establish a financial services company dedicated to guiding people towards prudent investments – and that is how I founded Microsec.

Now it's Your Turn!

The key takeaway from this *lokokti* is the immense value of diligent record-keeping. In today's world, it is easy to access software tools that provide comprehensive solutions. If you are just starting out, invest in basic accounting software. But as you grow, you will need high-scale software like an Enterprise Resource Planning (ERP) tool.

Beyond this, the proverb also emphasises real-time data analysis. Track your transactions consistently. That way, you can gain valuable financial insights and stay aligned with your business vision.

***

Chapter 14

Vyaapar badha, punji badha, badha ped saakhro, nyaasi tu vyaapar ko, kul ko diyo aasro

(व्यापार बढ़ा, पुंजी बढ़ा, बढ़ा पेड़ साखरो, न्यासी तू व्यापार को, कुल को दियो आसरो)

A wise saying on balancing growth with responsible stewardship

From Father to Son: Generational Wisdom

There once lived a young Marwari businessman. His father was a man of great wisdom. As the son's business began to grow, the proud father approached him one day. The wise old man shared a mantra that held the key to long-term success.

He said, "*Beta, vyaapar badha.* Let your business grow...

Punji badha. Let your capital flourish...

Badha ped saakhro. Let your goodwill multiply many times over...

But remember, *nyaasi tu vyaapar ko.* You must see yourself as a trustee of your business, not its owner...

Kul ko diyo aasro. That way, you will become a beacon of hope for your family."

True success, explained the father, lies in stewardship, not ownership.

The Implicit Lesson

The values the father imparted to his son are essential for the long-term health of any business. At its core, the proverb guides us to a holistic approach to business and community. It reminds us that entrepreneurial success goes beyond just personal gain.

As your business expands, so will your capital. You will market your products and services and eventually establish a strong brand identity. But always remember that these achievements are collectively realised through the support of the people around you.

Being a *nyaasi* (trustee) rather than an owner of your own business represents this shift in perspective. It is about viewing your business as a legacy to be passed on, not a personal asset to be exploited. It is about lighting the lamp of sustainability, not only for your immediate family but also your extended family — your team.

A long-term outlook is essential in this respect. Instead of chasing immediate profits, focus on building a sustainable enterprise that can weather economic storms and support future generations.

And above all, practise social responsibility. Your business should be a catalyst for uplifting your community and contributing positively to society at large.

A Window into My Experiences

I have come to believe that, beyond a point when your financial goals are achieved, the only purposes that remain for your business are to generate goodwill and establish a legacy. The principle of trusteeship reflects this reality.

At the time when I started Microsec, I used to invest in the stock market. On days when I made a profit of, say, ten lakh rupees, I felt like I had won an Olympic medal. But this feeling was not long-lasting. With time, as I was able to meet my basic financial goals, additional gains in investment no longer brought the same excitement.

Today, if I am given two scenarios – first, gaining fifty lakh rupees from my investments, and second, eating an organically grown papaya from my farm – the first does not have any impact on me. It does not contribute to my sense of fulfilment. In contrast, enjoying that papaya brings me genuine happiness. My entire day becomes brighter with its simple pleasure.

I believe human needs are driven by purpose. And when that purpose aligns with trusteeship, you continue to find joy beyond your basic financial needs. At present, I feel that my basic financial goals are met, so I focus on helping achieve the financial goals of my team, contributing to society, and supporting the nation. I align the purpose of my business with that of trusteeship. My business growth then becomes a means to achieve these broader goals, creating a sense of fulfilment.

Now it's Your Turn!

The proverb places priority on long-term sustainability over short-term gains. Here are a few steps you could take towards it:

1. Adopt a stewardship mindset, viewing your business as a means of benefiting others. Prioritise the well-being of your employees, community, and broader society. Evaluate how your business can contribute to social, environmental, or economic causes.

2. Once your business has reached a financially stable state, reassess its primary objectives. Consider how your business can contribute positively to society and leave a lasting legacy. Implement metrics to track your business's social contributions.

***

Chapter 15

Punji par byajj, dharma dharmi, byajj de munaafo, vyaapari ki karni

(पुंजी पर ब्याज, धर्मा धर्मी, ब्याज दे मुनाफ़ौ, व्यापारी की करनी)

———— ❖ ————

*An age-old wisdom on how to tell returns
and profits apart*

Beyond the Bottom Line

This is quite a powerful proverb that speaks to the true economic indicators of a business or its EVA (economic value addition). In any enterprise, there are primarily three kinds of resources you deploy. First, you deploy capital, that is your capital allocation. Second, you deploy your time, that is your time allocation. And third, you deploy your risk, that is your risk allocation.

The proverb here suggests that to determine your true business profit, you should measure your EVA – the extra profit that you make beyond what you could earn from a passive investment, like a bank fixed deposit. In simple terms, if you invest your capital in a fixed deposit, you earn interest at 7% per annum. But if you invest that capital in your business, and ultimately, your business generates, say, a 10% return per annum, your true profit is only 3%.

Obviously, we need to evaluate business profit over a longer timeframe, such as ten to twenty years, rather than yearly. Financial analysis tools like ROCE (return on capital employed) and ROE (return on equity) can help you in this regard.

The core message of the *lokokti* is that your ROE should be evaluated to assess your EVA, the true measure of profitability. It is the inherent religion (*dharma dharmi*) of capital (*punji*) to generate interest (*byajj*) and return to you. But true business acumen lies in maximising this return (*byajj de munaafo, vyaapari ki karni*).

A Window into My Experiences

This proverb has influenced my thinking to a great extent. When I read about Warren Buffet and his investing style, my philosophy towards the subject gained more depth. I should also mention a book from the house of McKinsey & Company – Strategy Beyond the Hockey Stick: People, Probabilities, and Big Moves to Beat the Odds – that I found particularly enlightening. The authors Chris Bradley, Martin Hirt, and Sven Smit did an excellent job at explaining the intricacies of strategic investing.

I understood how this wisdom could be applied to my own businesses. In my first venture, Microsec, we achieved a positive EVA every block of three years. However, in my second business, SastaSundar, we faced initial losses but ultimately generated significantly higher EVA in blocks of ten years.

This experience taught us the importance of calculating EVA over time blocks rather than calculating it year on year. It taught me that long-term strategic planning is crucial for truly understanding business success.

Now it's Your Turn!

In business, your most valuable resource is your time, and it gets compounded with every hour you put in. Your time allocation is seconded by your capital allocation. Consider the allocation of both of these resources very carefully because they have an opportunity cost. But I believe businesses are not built by staying at the seashore. Businesses are built by venturing into the sea and facing headwinds.

That's why, keep your EVA in mind, but always align your evaluation with your unique business purpose. The purpose may vary based on your industry, goals, or the very nature of the business you are building. For example, if you are in the hospitality industry and own a restaurant, you might expect to see profits after the first two years, followed by steady annual growth. If you decide to open a second restaurant, then also evaluate your profit only from the first restaurant, as it has matured and benefited from the compounding effect of your time. The new restaurant's performance should be assessed after it has had the same time to mature – typically two years.

Similarly, if you are building a tech startup, the evaluation should not be based on immediate profit but rather on the stage of development. Building a tech ecosystem in itself takes a lot of time. It is essential to assess your progress honestly, recognising that in some cases, you are building an ecosystem without a clear end result in sight.

To put it simply, if you are on a train journey from Kolkata to Delhi, you will not reach your destination immediately, but you should measure progress by ensuring you have crossed key stations like Durgapur or are at least approaching them.

***

Chapter 16

Karsu karsu gaathli, karni kade na aao, je karni sachri, jatan abhi batay

(कर्सु कर्सु गाठली, करनी कदे ना आव, जे करनी साचरी, जतन अभी बताय)

A proverb that appreciates the value of quick actions

The Prompt Factory President

Once upon a time, there lived a businessman, *Seth ji*, who owned a factory. The factory was located fifty kilometres away from the city, and it took *Seth ji* around two and a half hours to reach. So, he appointed a factory in charge who lived nearby. He was the factory's president.

One day, *Seth ji* visited the factory for a routine inspection. He noticed new reinforced fences surrounding the property. The boundary was approximately one and a half kilometres long and must have cost at least one and a half crore rupees. After examining it, he called the factory's president and expressed his disapproval. "While it is good that you have built the boundary," *Sethi ji* said, "sadly, the construction is subpar – it is small, low, and crooked. It needs to be rectified. Demolish it and rebuild it properly, or the investment will be wasted!" With that, *Seth ji* left the factory.

But it was only upon returning home after the two-and-a-half-hour journey that *Seth ji* realised the high cost of rebuilding the boundary. He considered modifying the existing fence with changes like repainting. He promptly called the president. "Hold on, my friend!" he said over the phone, "I know I asked you to rebuild the fence, but let me reconsider a bit more. I will get back to you with my decision." On the other side of the phone, the president hesitated. Finally, he replied, "But, *Seth ji*, I did not wait a minute after you left. We have already broken down the old fence, and the planning for the new one is underway." Though initially taken aback, *Seth ji* quickly composed himself – and ultimately – could not help but appreciate the president's swift action.

Karsu karsu gaathli, karni kade na aao – those who promise that they will act, never end up doing anything.

Je karni sachri, jatan abhi batay – but those who truly intend to do the work, always act immediately.

What Do We Learn

In the dynamic world of business, where markets fluctuate and competition is fierce, having a long-term vision is non-negotiable. However, a robust strategy is only as good as its execution. Your team's energy is what drives your business forward. Ensure this energy is fuelled by real actions, not empty promises.

On your business roadmap, set clear milestones and track your team's tangible progress towards those goals. Focus on what they are actually doing, not just what they say they will do. Those who truly aspire to succeed will not wait for tomorrow to take the actions needed now. The journey to long-term success begins with a single step today.

However, also appreciate the fact that success is not achieved in a single leap. It is a journey that requires consistent effort and attention to detail. Hence, it is important that you monitor the activities of your team over time, ensuring that they collectively contribute to realise the overarching strategy of your business. To put it simply, a vision without action is like a ship without a rudder. It may have a destination in mind, but it is unlikely to reach it. Make sure you have both the ship and the rudder.

A Window into My Experiences

Both at Microsec and SastaSundar, the team and I consistently adhered to the action taken before (ATR) process. This involved meticulous monitoring and documenting the serial number, action required, prime mover, support, target date, and review details for each task. To ensure accountability, we held weekly meetings that every team member was required to attend. We always designated one person as the prime mover, to prevent responsibility from turning into a football match where tasks are passed around without resolution.

We realised that it is important to assign tasks in a way that ensures that team members do not just become postmen passing the box along. Instead, they should actively own their responsibilities and complete them within the specified timeframe.

Now it's Your Turn!

Aim to build a culture of action, accountability, and results in your workspace. Here are some steps on how you can achieve it:

1. **Empower your team**: Delegate tasks based on each team member's strengths. Provide the necessary resources and guidance they need to succeed. Encourage them to take ownership of their work and make informed decisions.

2. **Foster a sense of urgency**: Establish clear deadlines for tasks and projects – communicate the importance of timely action. Recognise and reward employees who consistently exceed expectations.

3. **Lead by example**: Set realistic goals and achievable targets, so your team members can work effectively towards them. Avoid overcommitting on rewards; be cautious about making promises you may not be able to fulfil.

***

Chapter 17

Athanni gire toh khudhko hono chahiye

(अठन्नी गिरे तो खुड़कौ होनौ चाहिए)

———— ❧ ————

A wise saying on the importance of financial vigilance in business

The Sound of Money

I learnt about this *lokokti* during my service days at the Birla Building. The business there operated under a robust system known as the *parta* system. It ensured that every calculation was performed with absolute precision.

On the back of this system, a well-regarded saying circulated in the building: *Athanni gire toh khudhko hono chahiye.* If even a half-paisa falls, it should make a sound.

The Coin Dropped, but Did You Hear It?

A business thrives on the constant flow of transactions; money is its lifeblood. However, this constant movement also exposes you to risks such as loss, theft, and cash leakage. These incidents become an inevitable part of doing business.

It is understandable that you may not be able to prevent these incidents entirely, but you must have systems in place to detect them immediately.

Implementing robust internal systems, precise accounting practices, and effective control measures can help you catch even the smallest discrepancies in your finances. This vigilance is essential for safeguarding your business and ensuring its long-term success.

A Window into My Experiences

Having been trained at the Birla Building, I implemented the mechanisms of internal control and checks at both Microsec and SastaSundar from the very beginning. It is not that our businesses never experienced losses; it is not that there was never any theft or fraud. However, our proactive approach always helped us identify and address these issues promptly. This way, we were always able to catch the slippages early on – and that ultimately – helped us preserve our organisational values.

Now it's Your Turn!

Your business is a ship that traverses long distances in financial waters – both calm and stormy. Major occurrences like a raging storm (or an economic downturn), as well as minor incidents like a sudden gust of wind (or a small accounting error), are all part of the journey. What you, as the captain, need to do is stay informed and prepared for whatever may come. To ensure your vessel reaches its destination safely, here are a few steps you can take:

1. **Utilise technology:** Robust accounting software is like a reliable compass. It can guide you through the complexities of financial management. It automates processes, ensuring accuracy and efficiency. Fraud detection tools are your radar, scanning for potential threats lurking beneath the surface. Data analytics is your sonar, revealing hidden patterns and anomalies that could signal trouble.

2. **Implement infallible internal controls**: To protect your ship, you need a vigilant crew. Segregate duties, ensuring no one team member holds too much power. Document everything meticulously, like a ship's captain charting its course. Implement strong security measures, like locking the ship's hold. Regularly inspect for leaks, just as a captain would check for damage. And finally, train your crew to spot any unusual occurrences, like a strange noise or a suspicious package.

3. **Strengthen your financial reporting:** Empower your team to produce accurate and timely financial reports. Regularly reconcile your bank statements and other financial records, just as a navigator would check the ship's position against the stars. And analyse the data to identify trends and potential issues.

4. **Enhance your risk management process:** Just as a captain would survey the horizon for signs of storms, you need to identify potential risks to your business. Once you have pinpointed these threats, you can take steps to mitigate or eliminate them. Consider purchasing insurance coverage to safeguard your business from unexpected losses.

***

Chapter 18

Cha baar labh pasa ka, ayo gayo juwari, jeewan karam labh ka, bin khev vyaapari

(छ बार लाभ पासा का, आयो गयो जुवारी, जीवन कर्म लाभ का, बिन खेव व्यापारी)

An age-old wisdom on the consistency of profitability

Consistency, Consistency, and Some More Consistency

In the world of business, success is not defined by a single victory but by the ability to achieve and sustain it. This is reflected in the wisdom of a famous *lokoti* that says unless you win six times at dice *(cha baar labh pasa ka)*, it is not skill – it is gambling.

The first few winning rolls might be born of speculation or sheer luck. In the business space, there are many such gamblers who overestimate their abilities based on early profits (*ayo gayo juwari*). These short-term gains must not be attributed to intelligence or business acumen. True expertise is revealed through consistent performance, not fleeting victories.

Therefore, when evaluating a businessperson's skills, consider their business's long-term track record. Has its success been sustained over time? Has it demonstrated the ability to adapt to changing market conditions and overcome challenges? These factors, rather than short-term highs, are the true indicators of an established business ecosystem and an even more skilled businessperson (*jeewan karam labh ka, bin khev vyaapari*).

Is Your Profit – Casual or Sustainable?

Let's understand this through a story. Once upon a time, there lived a young entrepreneur A. Driven by a desire for quick success, he adopted a strategy of cutting corners and exploiting resources. His business thrived initially, raking in casual profits like a gambler hitting a lucky streak.

But as time went by, the consequences of the entrepreneur's actions began to show. His business became a house of cards. Customers complained about his substandard products, employees felt exploited, and environmental regulations were flouted. The entrepreneur's reputation took a nosedive, and his once-thriving business began to crumble.

Meanwhile, across town, another entrepreneur, B, was building her business on a foundation of sustainability. She invested in eco-friendly practices, treated her employees fairly, and prioritised ethical sourcing. Her business grew steadily, like a mighty banyan tree, rooted firmly in the ground.

Entrepreneur B's sustainable profit was not as immediate or flashy as Entrepreneur A's initial gains, but it was built on a solid foundation that would endure. This is the very difference between casual and sustainable profit.

And this brings us full circle to the teaching of our *lokokti* – consistency is key.

A Window into My Experiences

I have an interesting anecdote to share here. At Microsec, there was a time when we received both an investment banking mandate for an IPO (initial public offering) and a service request from a client simultaneously. This had us slightly puzzled. We debated in our general meeting whether we had acquired the mandate or the client. The unanimous conclusion was that we only secured the mandate. Until we received repeat business, we could not confidently say that we had successfully onboarded the client.

And so it went on for nearly a year; we regularly provided service to the client. Then, one day, something unexpected happened. The client called me and said, "Mittal *ji*, I have a favour to ask. I am sending you a girl's resume. Could you advise whether she would be a suitable match for my son?" I was surprised because this was not my area of expertise. I was all of thirty-five at the time and certainly no marriage counsellor! But despite everything, I promised the client that I would do my best to help him.

I brought the issue back to Microsec's general meeting. Again, the consensus was unanimous, but on a matter that was closer to home – Microsec had finally landed the client! We had become a trusted adviser, a habit, for the client. He now seeks counsel from us on critical life decisions. This trust was above and beyond mere transactions. It showed us why repetition and consistency hold so much value in business.

I also applied all these learnings at SastaSundar. There, we analysed customer data over a six-month timeframe. For instance, we monitored whether a customer consistently placed orders within a six-month window. Recognising the importance of repeat behaviour, we even designed a dedicated 'Reorder' button for our app. It proved to be a hit among our clients.

Now it's Your Turn!

The proverb serves as a cautionary tale against resting on your laurels. It spotlights the importance of sustained success and the need for continuous improvement. Here are some steps you can take towards it:

1. Monitor your order patterns closely. Are customers returning repeatedly and purchasing the same items? Or are they trying different products (or services) each time? Analyse customer behaviour to identify opportunities for optimising their experience in both scenarios.

2. If there are no repeat visits, the initial transaction might be a result of short-term factors like limited supply or high demand in the market. Evaluate how you can encourage customers to return.

3. Seek customer feedback. Ask both repeat and one-time customers about their experiences. Listen attentively to their feedback to determine if the transactions are due to chance or long-term value creation.

***

Chapter 19

Gidar ri maut aave, toh woh gaon k saam bhaage

(गिदड़ री मौत आवे, तो वो गांव क साम भागै)

---

*A wise saying on the importance of strategic thinking
in the face of fierce competition*

When it is the Jackal's Time to Die

In the animal kingdom, the jackal is known for its cunning nature. It approaches most situations with a sly attitude and an intent to kill. There is a popular Marwari saying that speaks to the jackal's eventual downfall. It says that when the jackal or *gidar* senses its death, it runs towards the village.

Jackals typically enter villages with the intent to harm crops, livestock, and humans. It goes without saying that the villagers retaliate. Hence, it is the jackal's greed, impatience, and, most importantly, underestimation of its adversaries that lead it to the village, and ultimately, to its death.

Beyond the narration of the jackal's misfortune, the proverb also offers a valuable life lesson. It teaches us to approach every situation with careful deliberation. No matter how much you want to win, always assume that your rival shares – if not surpasses – the same ambition. Impatience and greed have no place in the book of sustainable success.

In the face of intense competition, the wisest course of action is to play it safe and slow.

The Chanakya Niti Connection

Interestingly, the proverb also echoes Chanakya's teachings. The great Indian philosopher was the adviser to Chandragupta Maurya, the ruler of the Magadha empire. Once, Chandragupta launched an attack on the kingdom of Pataliputra, ruled by the mighty king Dhana Nanda. Chandragupta was severely defeated in that battle, losing much of his manpower and wealth.

Desperate for a new strategy, Chandragupta and Chanakya decided to venture out of the palace one day and regroup. They sought some fresh air and an even fresher perspective. While wandering through Magadha, they passed by a house where a mother was serving lunch to her young son. That day, the woman had cooked *khichdi*. Hungry and impatient, the little boy could not wait. He dipped his hand into the piping-hot vessel and badly burned his fingers. Unaware that Chandragupta and his trusted adviser were standing right at their doorstep, the mother reprimanded her son, saying, "*Beta*, don't be foolish like

Chandragupta and Chanakya. They were defeated in the battle because they attacked Dhana Nanda in the heart of Pataliputra… If you want to have your *khichdi* hot, eat from the side, not the middle."

From this analogy of the humble *khichdi*, Chanakya's eyes opened to an invaluable life lesson. If you lack the strength of your adversary, attack slowly and steadily from the side. This way, you can gradually gain a stronger position and eventually get to the middle.

In the context of business competition, this means outmanoeuvring a stronger rival rather than directly challenging them. This might involve finding new market niches, developing innovative products or services, or forming strategic alliances.

A Window into My Experiences

This *lokokti* has been a part of me from a young age. Naturally, I applied it in my business ventures, too. Before starting Microsec, we had many debates about the company's base location. For a while, we considered headquarters in Mumbai, but Mumbai has always been saturated with competition. It was and still is the centre of the proverbial hot *khichdi*. So, we recalibrated and started our journey from Kolkata instead. There, we were the only investment bankers at the time. We were able to secure our initial mandate very quickly, as a result.

Now it's Your Turn!

Imagine your business as a warrior on a battlefield – like Chandragupta Maurya. To emerge victorious, here are the first steps you must take:

1. Have a thorough understanding of your own strengths and weaknesses. A SWOT analysis (that is, the analysis of your strengths, weaknesses, opportunities, and threats) is like a battle plan, outlining your assets and vulnerabilities.

2. Next, assess your competition. Study their strategies, tactics and capabilities. Knowledge is power, and understanding your competitors is a tactical advantage.

3. Evaluate your resources. Are you equipped with the same weapons and armour as your rivals? If so, you can confront them head-on. However, if you are outmatched, consider a more strategic approach. Instead of charging directly into the fray, focus on building your competitive advantage and finding alternative paths to victory. Remember, the battlefield is dynamic, so adapt your strategy as circumstances change.

The above steps capture the very essence of Chanakya Niti. The philosopher's timeless wisdom teaches that failure is almost always inevitable without proper preparation.

***

Chapter 20

Saanch ko ke naap, sutli ko saanp

(साँच को के नाप, सुतली को सांप)

————— ✤✤ —————

A wise saying on the power of perception

The Laundry-Doing Friend

There is a famous humorous poem that often makes the rounds at *kavi sammelans*. It describes the playful banter between two friends – one of whom is recently married. The poem goes:

Mein dho raha tha kapde,

Ke mere yaar ne pucha,

Ye kaise hai laafde,

Shaadi ke baad yun rota hai,

Aapna pajama khud dhota hai!

Maine kaha, yaar teri aankhon mein khot hein,

Yeh pajama nahin, petticoat hai!

The poem paints a comical picture of a newlywed man doing his laundry. His friend, surprised at this unusual behaviour, teases him about being too attached to his pyjamas. The newlywed, in a playful retort, claims that those are not pyjamas, but a petticoat.

Beyond the frivolities, this light-hearted poem also has an important lesson to teach. It sets the stage for the proverb of this chapter.

Is it a Rope or a Snake?

Saanch ko ke naap. The truth cannot be measured.

Sutli ko saanp. Even a rope can be seen as a snake.

In the business field, the power of public perception is paramount. While it is essential to be honest and transparent, it is equally important to understand how your target audience perceives your products or services. If you play your cards right, your customers will see your offerings exactly as you want them to. Your marketing strategies play a key role in shaping this perception.

Customers pay for the brand as much as the product or service itself. If the perceived value of your offering is higher, people are willing to pay more. However, false information can spread like wildfire, distorting the truth and misleading consumers.

This makes it imperative to control your brand's perception. Create compelling narratives, employ effective marketing strategies, and ensure your messaging reaches and resonates with your target audience.

Think of it this way: imagine a brilliant diamond but with a rough, uncut surface. Its true value remains hidden until it is expertly crafted. Similarly, the power of truth lies not just in its existence but in how it is presented and perceived.

A Window into My Experiences

When we launched SastaSundar, our primary focus was on conveying a message of health and happiness through the delivery of genuine medicines. We aimed to establish a reputation for authenticity, not just affordability. While discounts were certainly a factor, they were not the core of our communication strategy.

In contrast, our competitors prioritised rapid growth through aggressive discounting. However, SastaSundar's continued commitment to genuine medicine enabled us to achieve sustainable growth, even with relatively lower discounts compared to our rivals.

Now it's Your Turn!

Turn your business's raw potential into a valuable and sought-after brand, just as a rough diamond is transformed into a precious gem. Start your journey from business to brand by asking yourself:

1. **What is my unique selling proposition?** Identify your business USP and the qualities that set you apart from your competitors. This is your diamond's rough form.

2. **What is my brand messaging?** Develop consistent, on-brand messaging that reflects your core values and USP. Create high-quality content that demonstrates your expertise and

showcases your diamond's value. This is the cutting process and your way to a strong brand identity.

3. **Who is my target audience?** Identify the right audience. A great offering means little if it does not reach the right ears. This is the polishing process. It makes sure that your diamond shines where it matters most.

4. **What can I do better?** Listen to the market intently. Consistently seek feedback from your customers and adapt your strategies accordingly to keep your diamond relevant and appealing.

***

Chapter 21

Taka toh tem ko tabar hai

(टका तो टेम को टाबर है)

*A timeless saying on time, money, and their
combined multiplier effect*

The Power of Compounding

Compounding is a powerful tool for wealth accumulation. It is the process of earning interest on both your initial investment and the accumulated interest. Put simply, it is letting your money work for you.

Here is an example to break down the concept:

Suppose you save fifteen thousand rupees per month for fifteen years, and it is compounded annually at a rate of fifteen per cent. You will have approximately one crore rupees at the end of the period. This is because the interest earned on your initial investment is added to your principal, and then interest is earned on the increased amount.

Now, if you continue to save fifteen thousand rupees per month for another fifteen years, your total savings will grow to approximately ten crore rupees at the end of thirty years. This significant growth is due to the continued compounding effect. The interest on your growing principal makes your savings multiply by about ten times.

So, after thirty years of saving fifteen thousand rupees per month at a fifteen per cent compound interest rate, your total savings will skyrocket.

This is the 15 x 15 x 15 theory of compounding, which spotlights the idea that if you start investing early and consistently, you can achieve remarkable financial growth over the long term.

Money is the Child of Time

Taka toh tem ko tabar hai – time is a precious commodity, and money is its offspring. When combined effectively, they can create a powerful multiplier effect through compounding.

In business, compounding is not just a financial concept; it is a strategic multiplier. Think of it as a catalyst that accelerates growth, turning small wins into monumental achievements.

The two single most important resources you deploy in your business are your time and capital. Time allows your money to grow through interest, while capital provides the initial investment that earns interest.

However, the limited nature of time is a big challenge. You have a productive working life of approximately twenty-five years during which you need to earn and save for your future.

This makes it essential to prioritise time over capital. You should start investing early and consistently, even if you can only invest small amounts initially. The power of compounding will take care of the rest.

A Window into My Experiences

I have seen firsthand how powerful compounding can be, both personally and professionally. For example, when my children were young, I started a tradition of gifting them sovereign gold bonds on their birthdays. Over time, these small investments grew into substantial funds that helped cover their higher education costs. The key, as always, was consistent saving – no matter how modest the amount.

In my business ventures with Microsec and SastaSundar, I embraced the principle of perpetual growth. At both companies, the core culture of 'Being Child' fostered a mindset of curiosity, adaptability, and a relentless pursuit of learning.

From the financial standpoint, we prioritised capital allocation to ensure that our investments yield maximum returns through compounding. We combined the strength of time and capital to build two robust businesses.

Now it's Your Turn!

Like in life and in business, time is money. Leveraging the power of compounding is like planting a seed and watching it grow into a mighty banyan tree. Here are some actionable steps to harness this multiplier effect:

1. **Start early, sow the seeds:** The sooner you start, the more time your investments have to grow. Make regular, even small, contributions to your investments to start with.

2. **Nurture the growth:** Select investments that align with your risk tolerance and financial goals. Spread your investments across different asset classes to mitigate risk. Regularly review your portfolio and make adjustments as needed.

3. **Use compounding to your advantage:** Familiarise yourself with how compounding works, and then let time work for you. Allow your investments to grow over the long term. Resist the temptation to withdraw funds prematurely, as this can hinder compounding.

***

Chapter 22

Arth bina vyarth hai, arth hi anarth hai

(अर्थ बिना व्यर्थ है, अर्थ ही अनर्थ है)

*A powerful proverb on the adequacy of capital and
its proper allocation in business*

Is Capital Always Good?

Businesses thrive on capital, but there are situations where it can be a double-edged sword. This fundamental tool for modern entrepreneurship can be both a saviour and a destroyer. Let's understand this through the lens of the *lokokti*.

When Capital is a Saviour

Capital is the fuel that powers the engine of business. Without sufficient fuel, even the most powerful engine will sputter and stall. Similarly, without adequate capital, even the most brilliant ideas and dedicated efforts will be unable to take flight. Your time and effort will be in vain.

Arth bina vyarth hai – Without capital, your ability to meet your personal and professional financial goals is severely limited.

However, money can bring happiness only to a certain extent. Once you have achieved your financial goals, the continued pursuit of money can prove to be detrimental to your overall well-being. The Indian concept of *santulan* teaches us the value of keeping balance and treading the middle path. This makes the theory of good enough crucial for both our daily life and business. It is important to remember that sometimes all we have is all we need.

When Money is a Destroyer

In business, overcapitalisation can pose a significant threat to long-term viability. While it might seem counterintuitive, having excessive capital can lead to a number of adverse consequences:

- **Indiscipline and waste:** When a business has more money than it needs, it can lead to a sense of complacency and a lack of financial discipline. Resources are wasted on unnecessary expenses.

- **Wrong practices:** Overcapitalisation can also encourage unethical or unsustainable business practices. With abundant funds, there may be a temptation to cut corners or prioritise short-term gains over long-term sustainability.

- **Vulnerability to market shifts:** Overcapitalised businesses can be particularly vulnerable to market fluctuations. If they are unable to adapt to changing conditions, the excess capital may not be enough to cushion the impact.

- **Loss of focus:** Excess capital can divert a business's attention from its core mission and values. When there is a surplus of funds, there may be a temptation to pursue unrelated ventures or expand into new markets without careful consideration.

Arth hi anarth hai – the pursuit of wealth can become an all-consuming obsession, overshadowing other important aspects of your business.

It is important for businesses, especially startups, to carefully manage their finances and avoid the pitfalls of excessive funding.

A Window into My Experiences

Throughout my business journey, two key principles have guided me: securing adequate funding and its strategic allocation.

In both Microsec and SastaSundar, whether working with tight budgets or managing larger sums, our focus has always remained consistent. We have ensured that every rupee spent is purposefully directed towards the right initiatives. This approach has helped us achieve sustainable growth while maximising the impact of our financial investments.

Additionally, we balanced our organisational needs with available resources, which gave us a clear understanding of how thoughtful funding decisions can drive long-term success.

Now it's Your Turn!

Money has a dual nature – it can prop you up or make you fall. Understanding and balancing this duality is important for long-term success. Here are some actionable steps you can take:

- **Shield yourself by avoiding excessive funding:** Seek only the capital you truly need and avoid overcapitalisation. Explore multiple revenue streams to reduce reliance on a single source.

- **Sharpen the blade with strategic planning:** Develop a clear business plan outlining your goals, financial projections, and risk management strategies. Promote financial literacy by educating yourself and your team about financial management principles.

***

Chapter 23

Jaha daata waha mangta, jaha mangal waha naad, jaha bhakt waha harikatha, jaha murkh waha vivaad

(जहां दाता, वहां मांगता, जहां मंगल, वहां नाद, जहां भक्त, वहां हरिकथा, जहां मूर्ख, वहां विवाद)

A proverb on the significance of environment in shaping outcomes, especially in business

The Universal Law of Attraction

In our personal and professional lives, all of us have a tendency to gravitate towards environments that mirror our own thoughts and behaviours. The proverb summarises this idea:

Jaha daata waha mangta – where there is a giver, there will be takers. People who are generous and giving often attract those who seek to receive.

Jaha mangal waha naad – where there is happiness, there will be melody. Joy and contentment create an environment conducive to creativity and expression.

Jaha bhakt waha harikatha – where there are devotees, there will be divine discourse. Places of worship and spiritual devotion are often filled with sacred teachings and a sense of divine presence.

Jaha murkh waha vivaad – where there are foolish people, there will be quarrels. Trivial arguments and disagreements are often found among those who lack wisdom or understanding.

The Importance of Environment

Our surroundings shape our thoughts, behaviours, and experiences. The company of like-minded individuals can create a supportive and enriching atmosphere while associating with those who do not share our values or beliefs can lead to conflict and frustration.

Similarly, a company's culture is the sum of its values, beliefs, and behaviours. The people you work with – your team, customers, and stakeholders – have a profound impact on your professional success. Collaboration with those who share your values promotes a positive and productive work atmosphere. On the other hand, working with those who have opposing goals can create tension and reduce productivity.

But There is Value in Constructive Debates

All of us desire to live in environments where people agree with and respect our ideas. But careful consideration will tell you that such environments can sometimes be limiting. A lack of diverse perspectives can stifle growth. So, engage in discussions with qualified individuals who hold viewpoints different from yours. By challenging your assumptions and learning from others, you can gain new insights and improve your decision-making.

However, choose your fellow debaters wisely. The quality of your conversations significantly impacts their outcome. They are valuable only when the dialogue is respectful and productive. Learn to distinguish between noise and music; engage in debates, not arguments.

A Window into My Experiences

At SastaSundar, we shaped our organisational culture around our core value of 'Being Genuine'. This commitment to authenticity is reflected in all our communication – whether with customers, employees, stakeholders, or vendors. This mindful strategy simultaneously reinforced our core values and created a cohesive and high-quality work culture.

Genuineness attracted genuine people to our organisation. It inspired us to engage in meaningful and authentic actions. Above all, it created a culture of authenticity that permeated our thoughts and practices.

Now it's Your Turn!

A thriving business is like a garden that requires constant care and attention. Invest in your company culture to create an ecosystem where everyone can flourish. Here are some actionable steps:

1. **Seek out synergies:** Identify and connect with stakeholders who share your company's values and goals. Build strong relationships with customers, suppliers, and investors. Collaborate with them to develop new ideas and opportunities. Exchange knowledge and experiences with them to improve your business practices. Within your workspace, recruit individuals who share your company's principles and passion. Conduct thorough interviews to assess potential candidates' cultural fit.

2. **Foster a garden of fearless innovation:** Provide a space where employees and external stakeholders feel comfortable sharing ideas without fear of judgment. Recognise and reward innovative contributions from all sources.

3. **Address conflicts with care:** Establish procedures for resolving conflicts in a respectful and constructive manner. Build a culture of open and honest communication to address concerns and disputes effectively.

***

Chapter 24

Taka katori sakh samandar

(टका कटोरी साख समंदर)

A wise saying on the interconnectedness of capital and reputation in business

The Ocean and the Bowl

In business, the two most important markers of growth are your capital and goodwill. This chapter's proverb illustrates this metaphorically:

Taka katori – capital is like a bowl full of water.

Sakh samandar – goodwill is the ocean from which that water is drawn.

In essence, the proverb assigns a higher value to your reputation compared to your capital resources.

The underlying logic is simple: money or capital is generated through goodwill. Without a solid reputation in the market, attracting customers and investors becomes a challenge. However, with a strong reputation, you can continuously scoop capital from an endless ocean of goodwill.

You Can Drink from the Bowl, But Can You Drink from the Ocean?

Contrary to what I said above, you might think that reputation only matters when you have the capital, to begin with. Having a long-term vision is key. Reputation is not about instant gratification; it is about building wealth over time. In the long run, you need both – money and goodwill. So, do not put yourself in a position where you have to choose between the two.

However, if you must choose, always remember that your reputation holds greater value. It is the foundation of your survival. With a strong reputation, even if you lose everything, you can always rebuild. The reverse, however, is not true.

That said, the ideal approach is to have both – money and reputation. In business, it is important to keep your access open to both the bowl and the ocean.

Follow Chanakya's Footsteps

I will again share a story from Chanakya's life as an example. The great Indian philosopher helped Chandragupta Maurya ascend to the throne of Magadha and became the king's chief adviser. However, Chanakya's straightforward methods earned him many enemies in the royal court. One such enemy, a minister named Rakshasa, spread rumours and false accusations against him.

Though Chanakya was extremely wealthy by then, he knew that his reputation as a wise and incorruptible adviser was more valuable than any material wealth. To counter the attacks, Chanakya did not defend himself publicly; instead, he strategically used his wealth and resources to help the people of the kingdom. He funded public works, alleviated poverty, and supported farmers in times of crisis. His good deeds quickly overshadowed the false rumours and his reputation as a man of wisdom and integrity was restored.

By using his wealth for the greater good, Chanakya demonstrated that while money is important, reputation is the true foundation of power and influence. In the long run, his reputation not only safeguarded his position but also allowed him to continue guiding the empire. Just like in the *lokokti*, he kept drawing water from the ocean of his reputation, proving that goodwill can sustain a person even when capital is at risk.

A Window into My Experiences

One of the key principles behind founding Microsec was reputation. Clients shared their data and wealth management plans with us, so they needed to have confidence in us. For this, we needed strong goodwill. In the Indian IT ecosystem, you will notice that foreign clients trust companies like TCS and Infosys because they believe their data will be safe with them. We were inspired by these two companies, and we followed in their footsteps at Microsec.

For SastaSundar, we founded the organisation on the core value of 'Being Genuine'. In the Indian market, many medicines are fake or counterfeit. We created SastaSundar to address this. After our company launched, there was a discount war in the market. But even in that, we were able to survive with a comparatively lower discount due to our strong reputation as a supplier of genuine medicines.

Over time, we have learnt that genuineness and good intent are the keys to success. If you have these values, you always win at the business negotiating table. People will respect you, and because of that respect, business deals will work in your favour.

Now it's Your Turn!

Goodwill is the anchor that keeps your ship steady in the stormy ocean of business. But capital is the bowl of water that can keep you going even in the most trying of times. Here are some actionable steps to help you balance both:

1. **Cultivate deep relationships:** The ocean is vast, but it is the connections we make that matter most. A positive reputation has a ripple effect. It attracts customers, investors, and talent. It can also lead to referrals and word-of-mouth marketing.

    So, build strong relationships with all your stakeholders and nurture the bonds with genuine care and understanding.

2. **Handle storms with strength:** Business is a journey filled with storms. Some are unexpected, and others are inevitable. But it is how you weather these storms that defines you.

    Be proactive in identifying potential crises and developing a plan to address them. This shows your preparedness and can help mitigate damage to your reputation.

    If a crisis occurs, respond promptly and with empathy. Acknowledge the situation, apologise if necessary, and take immediate steps to resolve the issue.

View challenges as opportunities for growth and never lose sight of your long-term goals. Courage in the face of adversity is a valuable asset for any leader.

3. **Measure and monitor:** Use online tools and surveys to monitor your reputation. Pay attention to customer feedback and social media sentiment. If you identify areas where your reputation is suffering, take steps to improve it. This may involve addressing negative reviews, changing your business practices, or launching a public relations campaign.

***

Chapter 25

Ginti ki chaal, rana ki dhaal

(गिनती की चाल, राणा की ढाल)

A proverb on the importance of careful planning and strategy, akin to a king's protective shield

Is Doing Business a Risky Business?

If you are an established business or aspiring to be one, you likely have faced a common question from your family, friends, and even acquaintances, "Stop thinking about it! Doing business is a risky business!" And from the outside, they are not entirely wrong.

Business does involve a lot of groundwork, from securing capital to investing the most productive years of your life, building and maintaining goodwill from scratch, and much more. The list of things you need to do scales as your business does.

But here is an insider's perspective: stop listening to misconceptions.

Business is not about taking risks; it is about managing risk. Just as nuclear energy can be harnessed for destruction or power, business decisions can lead to either.

Strategic Moves are Your Shield

Imagine your business as a battlefield. Every day, you are engaged in a series of skirmishes, each a small battle in the larger war for market dominance. Grand victories are reassuring, but it is the countless small victories that ultimately lead to success.

How do you achieve this? Successful businesses do not thrive on reckless gambles. Instead, they excel at calculated risk management. They know that in order to win tomorrow, they have to survive today first.

So take small, calculated steps. Think big about your goals, but start small and gradually scale your operations.

Ginti ki chaal, rana ki dhaal – Strategic moves are your armour of protection on the battlefield of business.

A Window into My Experiences

From my student days, I made it a priority to maintain a financial safety net. When I began my journey in chartered accountancy, my monthly expenses were around three thousand rupees. I always ensured that my savings account had at least that amount in surplus to cover the next month's expenses.

I applied the same principle at Microsec, where we took small, cautious steps while maintaining a big vision. We were building a large company, but our focus was on improving incrementally each day. Initially, the growth felt slow, but over a decade, the power of compounding helped us expand rapidly.

We then applied the principle at SastaSundar, too. Building a business is a long journey; breaking it down into manageable parts helped us avoid major setbacks. Our strategy of focusing exclusively on Eastern India was a deliberate, calculated move – our *ginti ki chaal*.

This approach allowed us to establish leadership in one region while shielding ourselves from aggressive tactics, like unsustainable discounting by competitors with deeper pockets. By concentrating our efforts, we achieved meaningful penetration, built a robust foundation, and positioned ourselves for sustainable growth in the future.

Now it's Your Turn!

Think big, act small.

Every business faces challenges, but with strategic thinking and careful planning, even the smallest enterprises can succeed. Here are some actionable steps:

1. **Always have a Plan B:** Be prepared for setbacks by having contingency plans in place, so you are ready to pivot when needed.

2. **Use guerrilla tactics:** Small businesses often have an advantage over larger corporations: agility. Use your flexibility to outmanoeuvre competitors and seize unexpected opportunities.

3. **Fortify your defences:** Protect your business from threats by building a strong foundation. This might involve investing in cybersecurity, developing contingency plans, or establishing a loyal customer base.

4. **Learn from past mistakes:** Analyse your successes and failures. Understand what worked and what did not. Apply these lessons to future campaigns.

***

Chapter 26

Kehen ki kala, haath le ghanaa

(कहण की कला, हाथ ले घणा)

———✦———

A smart saying on the power of effective communication

The Art of Communication

Words alone hold meaning, but the right strategy transforms them into effective communication. Let's explore this idea through a story.

The Man Who Fell in the Gutter

Once upon a time, there lived a miserly man in a village in Rajasthan. One day, on his way to work, the man fell into a gutter in the middle of the village. Despite the man's reputation, the villagers shared a strong camaraderie with him. They quickly gathered around the gutter to pull him out. "Give us your hand, *bhaai sahab*, give us your hand," cried the villagers in unison, extending their hands. The gutter was not particularly deep, but it was proving quite challenging to pull the man out. The miser was not responding to the villagers; it was as if he either could not hear them or did not want to be saved.

Eventually, the crowd started growing weary and soon was almost ready to give up. It was only then that one of the villagers had a brilliant idea. "Listen, everyone!" he exclaimed. "This man is a miser. Perhaps he is not understanding our message. We need to adjust our approach to match his mindset."

Hearing this, understanding dawned upon the villagers. They unanimously started saying, "Take our hand, *bhaai sahab*, take our hand!" Pulling the miser out of the drain was only a matter of minutes after that.

Kehen ki kala, haath le ghanaa – the art of speaking is the key to being understood.

What Do We Learn

If your product or brand is an arrow, then communication is its bow. The arrow, no matter how well-crafted, will miss its target if the bow is not aimed correctly. Similarly, your product or brand will not resonate with your customers if you do not communicate in a way that they understand and appreciate.

A Window into My Experiences

When we started building the brand for Microsec, we were a very small company competing with much larger firms that had an established presence across India. We discussed how to effectively communicate with both our current and potential customers in a way that would position the Microsec brand strategically. That is when we developed our campaign to fit into the consumers' minds.

We noticed that other companies were talking about big things, so we created a simple slogan:

Small things matter. You listen to Microsec because we listen to you.

The message was straightforward – we were small, and that meant we placed a lot of value on supporting our clients. This slogan was a hit, and soon, we started acquiring customers.

At SastaSundar, we built our messaging around genuine medicines because people were highly concerned about the quality of medicines available in the market. We conveyed this directly with our slogan:

SastaSundar is health and happiness.

And people connected with it.

The key is to communicate what your customers want to hear, and that communication must be differentiated from the rest.

Now it's Your Turn!

The goal of communication is to connect with your audience. Here are some actionable steps you can take towards it:

1. **Understand your audience:** Identify your target audience. Who are they? What are their needs, wants, and pain points?

By understanding your audience, you can aim your message directly at them.

2. **Define your message:** Craft a clear and compelling message. What is the core value proposition of your product or brand? What makes it unique? Sharpen your arrow with a well-defined message.

3. **Choose the right channels**: Select the most effective channels to reach your audience. Consider their preferences and habits. Are they more likely to engage with written content, visual content, or audio content? Choose the right bow for your arrow.

4. **Tell a story:** People are more likely to remember and connect with stories. Use storytelling to illustrate the benefits of your product or brand. Add feathers to your arrow by weaving a compelling narrative.

5. **Be authentic:** Be genuine and authentic in your communication. People can spot inauthenticity from a mile away. Make sure your arrow is true by being genuine.

6. **Test and measure:** Experiment with different communication strategies to see what works best. Track your results and make adjustments as needed. Practise your archery and refine your communication skills.

7. **Focus on differentiation:** Imagine planting a mango tree and then spending millions to identify it – this is not a smart strategy, especially if it is in a garden full of mango trees. The same logic applies to your communication. In a crowded marketplace, your messaging must stand out. True

differentiation in communication comes from a distinct value proposition. However, even the strongest value proposition will be overlooked if it is not communicated properly.

***

Chapter 27

Chako ghumto pako

(चको घुमतो पको)

A proverb on the importance of grit and perseverance in business

The Story of Kumarapala

Kumarapala was a minor prince in the Chaulukya dynasty with little hope of ever becoming king. The ruling monarch was his cousin, Jayasimha Siddharaja, and Kumarapala lived in constant fear of being killed as a potential threat.

Despite the odds stacked against him, Kumarapala wanted to become king one day. He sought the guidance of Acharya Hemachandra, a Jain sage known for his wisdom in politics, governance, and economics. Hemachandra, seeing Kumarapala's potential, advised him to be patient. He taught the young prince that the wheel of life is always turning – what falls will rise again, but only for those who persevere and prepare for their moment.

Kumarapala lived in exile for years, gradually building support among those disillusioned with Jayasimha's rule. After the king's death, he seized his chance. Through careful planning and patience, he ascended to the throne.

Once king, Kumarapala's challenges were far from over. The kingdom he inherited was rife with internal strife, financial instability, and external threats. Hemachandra's advice was to continue applying his learnt principles: adapt to changing circumstances, focus on long-term goals, and prioritise the kingdom's well-being over short-term gains.

Kumarapala took this advice and worked tirelessly to stabilise the economy. His reforms targeted the kingdom's agriculture, taxation system, and trade. Under his rule, the Chaulukya dynasty (present-day Gujarat) became a centre of commerce and prosperity.

Chako ghumto pako – the wheel of life continuously turns through cycles of good times and bad.

Perseverance, Resilience, and Eyes on the Long Run

Kumarapala's journey from a hunted prince to a prosperous king shows how periods of hardship and adversity can be followed by success if one remains determined.

This principle is similar to business, where market conditions, competition, and external factors like economic downturns can impact success. Resilience is essential in such environments.

Consider how companies like Apple have faced numerous challenges, from financial struggles to intense competition, yet their focus on innovation and quality has helped them overcome barriers and emerge stronger.

Similarly, despite early setbacks, Netflix never lost sight of its long-term vision. The company's commitment to innovation and adaptability helped it transition from a DVD rental service to a global streaming giant.

A Window into My Experiences

When we launched Microsec in the early 2000s, everything went smoothly – until 2008, when the global economic crisis hit and nearly wiped out our entire net worth. At that point, we could have closed the shop, but instead, we decided to speed up. By 2010, we had recapitalised and successfully launched an IPO (initial public offering). However, another market crash soon followed, and our business began to lose relevance once again.

That is when we made the decision to pivot and launch SastaSundar. But the road was far from easy. In 2017, we faced a new challenge: competitors with deep pockets were burning cash and raising massive amounts of capital, making it increasingly difficult for us to secure funding. The market was consumed by discount wars, yet we refused to back down.

Then in 2020, the Coronavirus pandemic hit, and the discount wars finally eased. This also brought us a significant opportunity: a partnership with Flipkart Health Plus.

Through it all, the concept of *chako ghumto pako* became our guiding philosophy. There were moments when we had to slow down, but we never came to a stop. We kept the wheels turning, knowing that eventually, the rough roads would smooth out, the skies would clear, and we would be able to accelerate towards success.

Now it's Your Turn!

Your business is a river. Just as the water body keeps flowing to stay vibrant and healthy, your business needs continuous effort to thrive, regardless of the obstacles you encounter. Here are some actionable steps to help you:

1. **Keep the river flowing:** Regularly assess and streamline your processes. Invest in tools and systems that automate repetitive tasks, boost productivity, and keep the operational flow smooth. For example, adopting a CRM system can help manage customer interactions seamlessly, ensuring that no opportunities are lost due to miscommunication.

2. **Adapt to the changing terrain:** Stay agile and responsive to market changes. Conduct regular market research to understand emerging trends.

   When challenges become overwhelming, it is wiser to slow down and move carefully rather than stop entirely. Just as the river may alter its path to avoid obstacles, your business can shift direction while keeping its core intact. It should maintain a steady current, while your product lines can adjust like the river's branches, changing course as necessary.

   If certain branches dry up, it does not mean the river stops flowing. Close unproductive areas and redirect your energy towards channels that show more promise.

3. **Celebrate the rapids**: Recognise and build on your successes. Just as a river's rapids are exciting and signify strength, your business milestones and achievements should be celebrated to boost morale and drive further success.

***

Chapter 28

Tan bhagwaan ko, dhan samaaj ko

(तन भगवान को, धन समाज को)

*A timeless saying about balancing health and wealth
in life and business*

What Belongs to the Almighty

The *lokokti* of this chapter captures the ultimate theory of life and
the purpose of doing business. Let's break down the proverb and
explore its meaning, piece by piece.

The first part of the proverb, *tan bhagwaan ko*, means to pour
your heart and soul into serving the divine. You enrich your soul
and find purpose in your work when you dedicate your labour
and energy to a higher power or cause.

What Belongs to Society

The second part, *dhan samaaj ko*, translates to invest your wealth in the well-being of others. It urges you to open your heart and your purse for the betterment of society. It asks you to use your financial resources to uplift those in need, making a tangible difference in their lives.

Together, this proverb teaches us that our most meaningful contributions come from a place of love and selflessness. It invites us to merge our resources with our deepest values, creating a legacy of compassion that touches both the divine and the human spirit.

What Do We Learn

Health and wealth are both paramount aspects of a fulfilling life. Our bodies are gifts from a higher power, and regardless of our achievements, we must all face the inevitability of death.

Initially, we may engage in business to build a home, fund our children's education, or establish a legacy. However, once these aspirations are fulfilled, the marginal value of wealth becomes zero or even negative.

What remains is the deeper purpose of continuing to work: contributing to the greater good.

This idea aligns with the theory of enough and echoes the sentiment of the proverb – dedicating our physical efforts to a higher purpose and our wealth to societal welfare. Warren Buffett exemplifies this balance. Despite his age, he remains one of the wealthiest individuals in the world. His ongoing success stems from the power of compounding and the value of reinvesting in personal growth and the community.

A Window into My Experiences

I live by this *lokokti*. Let me share two simple examples from my life.

Buying my first car was pivotal for me – it marked a significant transition from using public transport to owning a private vehicle. Even though it was a small car, having my own air-conditioned vehicle felt like a life-changing upgrade. But when I later bought a bigger car, it did not bring the same excitement or sense of transformation. It did not significantly impact my sense of comfort or improve my life in a major way.

The same thing happened with my first home in Kolkata. The joy of owning that first house, the pride of having a place to call my own, was unparalleled. But later, when I bought a bigger house, the feeling was not the same – it did not touch my heart the same way.

In this journey of life, I have learnt that once we achieve our financial goals, there can be a sense of emptiness if our work lacks a greater purpose. When it is only about accumulating more money or possessions, the meaning gets lost. What has kept me motivated in business all these years is the drive to innovate and, more importantly, to serve – whether it's society, the nation, or the environment. It is this deeper purpose that truly fulfils me.

Now it's Your Turn!

Strive to strike a balance between health, wealth, and the greater good. Here's how you can align your actions with the proverb's wisdom:

1. **Take care of your well-being:** First things first. Just as you dedicate yourself to the success of your business, it is crucial to take care of your own health. A healthy leader is more effective and resilient. Regular exercise, a balanced diet, and mental relaxation contribute to sustained energy and clear decision-making.

2. **Integrate purpose into business strategy:** Ensure that your company's mission makes far-reaching contributions. Beyond traditional Corporate Social Responsibility (CSR) activities, seek to make a genuine impact on your community. Identify local needs and develop programmes that address them, like educational support, environmental sustainability, or health initiatives.

    This alignment boosts your company's impact and provides you with a deeper sense of purpose and fulfilment.

3. **Reinvest in both personal and community growth:** As you achieve your business milestones, allocate resources to personal growth opportunities, such as further education or mentorship, while also supporting initiatives that benefit society. This balanced approach propels both personal and communal progress.

***

Chapter 29

Jathe koni puge belgadhi, bathe puge Marwari

(जठे कोनी पूगे बेलगाड़ी, बठे पूगे मारवाड़ी)

A smart saying on the role of exploration and resilience in business

Do You Know Where the Word 'Marwari' Comes From?

Marwari originates from Marwar, a region known for its harsh conditions – scarce water, limited food, and frequent diseases. Facing such adversity, the Marwaris had left their homeland empty-handed, fully aware of the challenges ahead. Understanding that even getting a glass of water required significant effort, they had set out on a journey driven by a strong will to survive.

But their migration was not just a search for sustenance. It was a quest for opportunity. They ventured wherever resources were available, working hard and showing remarkable resilience. This ability to adapt helped the Marwari community thrive in new markets and seize growth opportunities wherever they arose.

Today, anywhere you travel in India, you will find a Marwari living there.

The Importance of Mobility in Business

Jathe koni puge belgadhi, bathe puge Marwari – where even the bullock carts cannot reach, the Marwaris do.

In business, staying still is as good as moving backwards. Many entrepreneurs fear stepping out of their comfort zones, but true progress demands boldness. Mobility is more than just physically moving from one place to another; it is about being open to change, exploring new opportunities, and breaking away from familiar routines.

It opens the door to fresh revenue streams and new customer bases. It helps you quickly adapt to new trends, technologies, and consumer demands. It ensures that your business remains relevant and competitive.

Consider how the Marwaris thrived by venturing into new regions and facing challenges head-on. Similarly, businesses that value adaptability are better equipped to seize opportunities and overcome obstacles.

A Window into My Experiences

I live in Kolkata, a city where having a stable job is highly valued. When I started working with Birla Corporation, with its good salary, company vehicle and housing, it seemed like the perfect setup. Yet, my father would always urge me to start my own business. His constant push for me to pursue change and growth reflected the Marwari spirit he had instilled in me.

So, despite the security and comfort, I left my job and started on an entrepreneurial path. I began as a tax practitioner, then expanded into multi-purpose service solutions, and eventually ventured into financial services with the launch of Microsec. However, by 2012, my team and I saw the need for a new direction. This led to the creation of SastaSundar, a digital healthcare platform. Seeing it succeed over the years confirmed the need for transformation.

My overall journey has taught me the value of adapting to change. I studied in Danta, a village in Rajasthan's Sikar district. If I had stayed there, I might never have reached this point in life. Moving to Kolkata was a leap of faith that led me to become a chartered accountant, gain independence, and tap into a bigger market.

Now it's Your Turn!

This is my favourite fact in business: success comes when opportunity meets preparation. If your current situation is fulfilling and aligned with your efforts, there is no need to change just for the sake of it. But if you find yourself unfulfilled or are not making the progress you hoped for, do not be afraid to adapt.

Here are some actionable steps to help you:

1. **Expand into new markets:** Consider expanding your business into new geographical areas or industries. For example, if you are running a local retail store, explore online sales channels or branch out to different cities. This expansion can open up new revenue streams and increase your market share.

2. **Embrace technological advancements:** Technology is a vehicle that can move your business forward. For instance, if you are not yet using data analytics, consider implementing tools like Google Analytics or CRM systems to gain insights into customer behaviour and improve your decision-making.

3. **Diversify your offerings:** If you run a restaurant, for example, consider adding a delivery service or launching new menu items based on customer feedback. This diversification can attract new customers and increase revenue.

***

Chapter 30

Baniyo teen jagah desi – baat mein, khat mein aur aat mein

(बाणियो तीन जगह देसी – बात में, खाट में और आंठ में)

---

*A wise saying on the three core qualities of
a successful trader*

The Art of Being Rooted

Marwaris, especially the Baniya business class, are famous for their entrepreneurial spirit and keen sense of commerce. The *lokokti* captures this ethos beautifully. Let's break down its elements and understand how it applies to the broader business landscape.

Baat mein desi

At the heart of successful businesses is the principle of trust, which is essential for building sustainable value. This is especially true for larger brands, like Apple, Jaguar, and Nike, whose high margins are supported by the goodwill they have earned over time. These companies thrive by cultivating a sense of pride in ownership. The key to their success lies in the impression they leave in the minds of their customers.

This same principle applies to traditional business practices, especially within the Marwari community, where trust is the cornerstone of every transaction. A Marwari businessperson's word is as valuable as any legal document. When a Marwari promises to deliver, he honours that promise – *pran jaye par vachan na jaye* – a saying deeply rooted in the community's ethos, which means a person may lose his life, but never his word.

Historically, Marwari businesspeople have followed this unwritten rule by heart. In Indian metropolitan cities like Delhi, Mumbai, and Kolkata, this ethos finds expression in a traditional lending practice known as *rukka*. A *rukka* is essentially a loan given on a simple piece of paper without the formalities of modern banking agreements. While bank loans may default, there is an unspoken rule that a *rukka* must always be repaid. It is seen as a personal commitment rather than a financial transaction, which holds deep significance in business circles.

Baat mein desi – so a skilled businessperson is known not only for their financial acumen but also for their ability to communicate clearly and honestly.

The tale of Nani Bai Ro Mayro often arises in conversations on this topic.

A story where one's word is a sacred bond

Nani Bai Ro Mayro is a famous Marwari folk tale that exemplifies the values of commitment and faith. The story centres around Narsi Mehta, a poor Brahmin and devotee of Lord Krishna, who promised a grand wedding for his daughter Nani Bai, despite lacking the means to fulfil it. Relying on his deep faith, he trusted Lord Krishna would provide.

On the day of the wedding, Lord Krishna, disguised as a wealthy merchant, miraculously arranged a lavish event, honouring Narsi Mehta's word. This tale praises the belief in the sacredness of a promise and the power of faith.

Khat mein desi

Now, onto the second part of the proverb.

Health is an area where people often have no choice but to rely on external help, especially when illness strikes. When someone is bedridden due to illness, they are faced with the inevitable costs associated with healthcare, such as doctor fees, surgeries, medications, and treatments.

In these moments of vulnerability, the need for healthcare becomes essential and non-negotiable. This creates both a financial and emotional dynamic where people are willing to invest whatever it takes to regain their health. As a result, healthcare services naturally generate significant value. Doctors, hospitals, and pharmaceutical companies play a key role in this ecosystem.

At the same time, businesses involved in healthcare are presented with opportunities to contribute to this vital sector in ways that are not only profitable but also impactful.

Khat mein desi – skilled business people understand the importance of serving people when they are most in need.

Aat mein desi

Successful businesses are those that solve real problems. Whether it is addressing the needs of individual consumers, contributing to national development, or solving broader societal challenges, businesses that focus on providing genuine solutions are the ones that create a lasting impact.

A great example of this is Tesla. The company has thrived by addressing both consumer and national concerns about sustainability and clean energy. By producing electric vehicles (EVs) that are stylish, fast, and increasingly affordable, Tesla solved a real problem: reducing carbon emissions while offering consumers an exciting, high-performance alternative to traditional cars.

Aat mein desi – skilled business people thrive when they stay true to solving real-world problems.

What Do We Learn

The proverb guides us in navigating both life and business with a blend of tradition and practicality. Its *desi* essence embodies a commitment to hard work and a forward-looking perspective, reminding us to stay rooted in our cultural values, even as the world evolves.

This mindset also spotlights the importance of creating a strong customer value proposition. In today's competitive market, businesses that focus on delivering genuine value are more likely to build loyalty and achieve sustainable success.

A Window into My Experiences

Throughout my business journey, my team and I have always prioritised creating compelling value propositions. When we started Microsec, we focused on two fundamental elements: building trust and solving real problems. We were *desi aat mein*.

To meet our customers' needs effectively, we created a capital pool by raising funds through both debt and equity. This financial strategy helped us to be agile and responsive; whenever there were capital issues, we could step in and provide the necessary support.

As we transitioned to developing SastaSundar, our primary goal was to address the pervasive issues of counterfeit and overpriced medicines. The core of our value proposition became offering genuine medicines at genuine prices. The concept of *khat mein desi* perfectly aligned with our mission.

And finally, the essence of *baat mein desi* tied all our operations. It became clear that our efforts went beyond simply selling products or services; our goal was to build trustworthy relationships.

Now it's Your Turn!

Be in the right place at the right time, taking the right action. The proverb offers three key strategies for success:

1. **Build goodwill and brand value**: Boosting your brand's reputation can differentiate you from competitors. For example, buying a luxury car not only adds to your personal satisfaction but also boosts your business's image. It becomes a symbol of success and pride, reflecting positively on your brand. Goodwill, in this sense, becomes a powerful asset that builds trust among customers.

   However, the opposite can also hold true. Some people prioritise simplicity as their core value. In India, for example, excess wealth can sometimes be perceived negatively. Those who live without modern conveniences, such as monks, often command great respect. Therefore, whatever your value proposition is, remain consistent in embodying that value across all aspects of your professional and personal life.

2. **Cater to personalised markets**: Personalised approaches create more value. Businesses that focus on direct connections with customers tend to be more sustainable, as long-term success relies on cultivating a large and loyal customer base.

   For instance, the proverb talks about the healthcare sector. But the logic applies to any customer-oriented industry. By tapping into a thriving space, you can meet demand while offering solutions that align with people's willingness to spend.

3. **Solve a meaningful problem**: Ultimately, if your business solves a real problem, customers will pay for it. In today's startup-driven culture, the companies that thrive are those that offer solutions to pressing issues. Customers are willing to pay for services or products that make their lives easier, more efficient or healthier.

***

Chapter 31

Jo kare beta faatka, woh ghaar ka na ghaat ka, uske rahe na katori na baatka

(जो करे बेटा फाटका, वो घर का ना घाट का, उसके रहे ना कटोरी ना बाटका)

An age-old wisdom on effective risk management

A Father's Insights on Taking Risks

Once there lived a father and son. As the son grew older, the father noticed that he had started casual gambling in the stock market. Concerned about the path his son was taking, the father decided to have an important conversation. One day, he approached the son and said,

"Listen son, those who speculate and gamble – *Jo kare beta faatka...*

They end up losing their place both in their own homes and society – Woh ghaar ka na ghaat ka...

More often than not, they find themselves in a situation where they have to sell their utensils just to survive – *Uske rahe na katori na baatka.*"

The father's words carried deep wisdom.

In the stock market, it is important to distinguish between speculative trading and genuine investing. Speculative trading often involves making quick trades based on market fluctuations, trends, or rumours, with the hope of earning quick profits. This approach can be highly risky and unpredictable. Research indicates that a large number of people who engage in speculative trading ultimately lose money. In contrast, genuine investing focuses on long-term growth and stability, through careful research and analysis. This approach tends to yield more sustainable results and minimises the risks associated with market volatility.

And doing business is no different.

The Segue into Business

Business is all about taking smart, calculated decisions. Instead of going after quick wins, successful entrepreneurs focus on really understanding their market. They dig deep into research, analyse opportunities and make choices based on solid strategies.

Doing business has never been about taking blind risks. It is about managing those risks and being prepared for the challenges that come with them. This proactive approach protects your investments and positions you to seize opportunities that others might overlook.

A Window into My Experiences

With the time I have spent in the capital market, I have come to one very clear understanding: You cannot succeed in stock market investing without understanding it well.

True power of investing lies in compounding. When you put your money into solid, fundamentally sound businesses, you set the stage for substantial growth over time. This is where patience and a long-term perspective come into play.

On the other hand, speculation can lead to a very different experience. I have often felt the weight of anxiety and regret when engaging in speculative trading, especially when decisions are based on fleeting trends rather than solid analysis.

Moreover, with the rise of algorithm-based trading and related software applications, the need for skill and strategy in the market has become even clearer. Achieving success in these areas requires a deep understanding of market dynamics, data analysis, and effective risk management. Unfortunately, many people underestimate these complexities and often end up facing unfortunate financial consequences.

And the strategies that helped me successfully invest in the stock market helped inform my business decisions as well. Just as I sought fundamentally sound companies for long-term growth, I focused on building a robust foundation for my ventures.

Now it's Your Turn!

I would like to share two very strong lessons from my own life that have shaped my understanding of investing. They can also be your practical guide for enhancing your investment strategies.

1. **Follow the 10 by 1 rule**: The stock market is more about the risks of timing than about investing itself. A principle I find helpful in this regard is the 10 by 1 rule. It is a guideline that ties your investment strategy to your time horizon.

   For example, if you have funds to invest for the next ten years, consider investing the entire amount in high-quality companies. This long-term perspective helps you benefit from compounding and ride out market fluctuations.

   However, for shorter time frames, adjust your allocations accordingly. For example, if you plan to invest for nine years, you should allocate 10% of your funds to debt instruments (such as bonds or fixed deposits) and the rest 90% to the stock market. Likewise, if your investment horizon is five years, adjust the allocation to a 50-50 split between debt and stocks.

   However, if you need access to your money within the next year, it is best to avoid the stock market altogether. The stock market is not designed for those seeking immediate returns.

2. **Avoid speculation and gambling**: Gambling is making decisions based on luck rather than research and strategy. It can lead to significant financial losses. Instead, focus on disciplined investing that prioritises long-term growth and informed decision-making. Your financial future deserves more than mere chance – it deserves a well-thought-out approach.

***

Chapter 32

Hath mein sarso koni uge

(हाथ में सरसों कोनी उगे)

A timeless proverb on the role of patience in achieving business success

Growth and Time

This proverb highlights a simple truth: growth cannot be rushed. Both in our personal and professional lives, meaningful progress takes time and patience.

Let's understand it in detail.

Inspiration from the Bhagavad Gita

In the Mahabharata, Lord Krishna said to Arjuna, *"Karmanye vadhikaraste ma phaleshu kadachana."*

Focus on the journey of your actions rather than the destination of your outcomes. Immerse yourself in your karma; results are shaped by forces beyond your control.

This teaching inspires a sense of liberation – when we let go of our attachment to success or failure, we free ourselves to fully engage in our efforts, allowing for personal growth and resilience. With this mindset, we can face life's challenges with courage and find deeper fulfilment in our pursuits.

But for that, patience is a must.

Can Mustard Grow in Your Palms?

In agriculture, a mustard seed sown in the ground does not sprout overnight. It needs the right conditions, consistent care and an understanding of its growth cycle. Each day that passes is a step towards the harvest, meaning that its growth can neither be rushed nor forced.

Our proverb aptly says – *hath mein sarso koni uge* – meaning mustard seeds do not grow in your palms. You need to do all the groundwork and then patiently wait for the crops to grow.

Similarly, in the business field, processes take time to yield results. Just as it takes nine months for a child to develop in the mother's womb, significant achievements in your venture often require a considerable investment of time and resources. This is where adopting a growth mindset becomes essential. It involves recognising that while you can optimise your processes and streamline your operations, you cannot drastically shorten the timeline for meaningful growth. Patience and perseverance are key.

There will be challenging periods along the way, and sometimes you will need to endure unfavourable conditions. However, it is important not to lose hope. Your responsibility is to consistently push forward, take proactive steps and remain engaged in your efforts. That way, you can cultivate the resilience needed to thrive, turning every experience into an opportunity for learning and growth.

A Window into My Experiences

I experienced this *lokokti* firsthand when I passed my CA examination in 1992. My dream was to establish my own financial services company, but as a fresh graduate, I knew I needed guidance. When I consulted with seniors, they all offered similar advice: while it is great to have dreams and a clear purpose, I needed to invest time in training myself first. They suggested I take at least five to seven years to work in a large organisation and learn the ropes before venturing on my own. This path, they said, would be more fruitful and less risky.

Looking back, their advice was invaluable. I took the time to gain experience, and after a few years, I finally started my own business.

Throughout my entrepreneurial journey, patience played an equally important role. Building a business is much like a rollercoaster – it has its highs and lows. There were moments when everything seemed to click, and the business thrived, but there were also tough times when nothing went as planned.

And during those challenging periods, my perseverance is what kept me going. But I never sat back and waited for things to happen. I began focusing on the little improvements – the small wins that gradually added up over time. When you see those incremental steps forward, you know you are heading in the right direction.

But I also learnt to recognise when something was not working. Patience does not mean holding onto a failing strategy. Sometimes, despite all your efforts, things do not improve, and in those moments, it is essential to change direction. Patience, in this sense, is not passive – it is active and observant. It is about planting seeds, nurturing them, and knowing when to make adjustments to help them grow.

Every entrepreneur faces setbacks, but it is important to know the temporary challenges from a failing venture. It is up to you to assess whether your business has room to grow or if it is time to move on to something else.

Now it's Your Turn!

Your business is a fertile farmland. Cultivate a thriving environment where sustainable growth can take root, helping you reap the rewards of your hard work over time. Here are some actionable steps you can take towards this:

1. **Plant the right seeds:** Choose your initiatives wisely. Focus on projects and strategies that align with your core values and long-term goals.

2. **Nurture with care:** Allocate time and resources to support your initiatives. This means regularly monitoring progress, providing employee training, and building a positive work culture.

3. **Be patient for growth:** Set realistic timelines and milestones, recognising that immediate results may not always be visible. Use this time to refine your strategies and adapt to changing circumstances.

4. **Harvest wisely:** When the time comes to reap the rewards of your efforts, do so thoughtfully. Assess your achievements and learn from both successes and failures. This reflection will guide future planting and help you make informed decisions.

5. **Replant and continue the cycle:** Use your experiences to plant new seeds for future initiatives. Continuously innovate and seek new opportunities for growth, ensuring your business evolves with changing market conditions.

***

Chapter 33

Dhul ki dhul koni hoye

(धूल की धूल कोनी होये)

*A proverb on viewing adversity as a springboard
for new opportunities*

When the End is the Beginning

Dust cannot be further dust – the proverb of this chapter translates exactly to this. It throws light on a simple fact of life: when something has already reached rock bottom, there is nowhere to go but up. Just as in the stock market, where prices reach a floor before bouncing back, businesses can find resilience in tough times.

After every setback, a comeback is not just possible – it is inevitable!

The Natural Cycle of Ups and Downs

Business journeys, much like any other in life, come with their fair share of highs and lows. While the tough times are inevitable, they make the successes even more rewarding. Understanding that difficulties are often temporary will help you maintain focus and momentum. Just like the night yields to dawn, setbacks too have a limit.

When faced with adversity, ask yourself, "How much worse can this get?" This mindset shift will empower you. A person already submerged underwater cannot be further harmed by water. Likewise, you can find strength in knowing you have weathered worse storms.

In Rajasthan, there is a colloquial saying: "We dance in the rain." This metaphor beautifully sums up resilience in business. When the rain pours down, many might seek shelter, waiting for the storm to pass. But to dance in the rain means to embrace the moment, to find joy and freedom even amidst the chaos.

A Window into My Experiences

In my twenty-five years of experience in business and investing, I have discovered that some of the greatest opportunities arise during times of crisis. I witnessed this firsthand during the 2008 financial meltdown and again in 2020 with the COVID-19 pandemic. Every investment I made in the stock market during those downturns proved profitable.

The same holds true for my businesses. In 2008, Microsec, being a financial services company, faced a slowdown. But by 2010, it rebounded stronger than ever.

When the COVID-19 pandemic struck, uncertainty loomed not just for SastaSundar but for companies around the globe. However, we turned this challenge into a pivotal moment for growth. Thanks to the unique market dynamics at play, we attracted more business and new investors.

I have come to realise that every low will eventually rise again, and every high will encounter a dip – that is simply the nature of business. The real challenge lies in determining whether a downturn or upturn is temporary or part of a longer trend. For this, a clear vision as an entrepreneur is essential. It is your ability to handle these fluctuations that will determine your success in the long run.

Now it's Your Turn!

Navigating tough times requires a strategic approach focused on resilience, resourcefulness and connection. When faced with challenges, it is crucial to recognise the current state of your business and use it as a launchpad for growth. Here's a guide to rebuilding and sustaining momentum, even from the lowest points:

1. **Recognise the bottom and build up:** Understand that when you hit rock bottom, the only way is up. Acknowledge your current situation honestly and use it as a foundation for rebuilding. Conduct a thorough assessment of your business to identify areas for growth.

2. **Nurture meaningful connections:** Strengthen relationships with customers, suppliers, and stakeholders. When you are down, these connections can provide support and

opportunities for collaboration. Show your customers that you are committed to their needs, even in tough times.

3. **Manage your costs**: Review your expenses critically and eliminate unnecessary costs. Focus on operational efficiency to ensure that your resources are used effectively.

4. **Create a financial safety net**: Develop a robust financial plan that includes a reserve for unexpected downturns. Having a financial cushion can help your business withstand shocks and give you the flexibility to address uncertainties without panic.

***

Chapter 34

Phokat mein barkat koni

(फोकट में बरकत कोनी)

------- ❖ -------

A wise saying on the importance of building prosperity through continuous value creation

Measuring Real Success

True prosperity is never a result of chance or handouts – it is built on a solid foundation of a strong culture and a sustainable business model. When success is achieved without effort or investment, it often lacks the substance needed for longevity.

In this chapter, I have explored how real growth and enduring prosperity emerge from the core values of a business, driven by continuous effort, innovation, and a deep understanding of market demands.

But first – a small story.

The King's Gift to the Woodcutter

Once upon a time, there was a kingdom ruled by a wise and graceful king. To better understand the true condition of his kingdom, the king would often walk around and meet his subjects.

One day, during his usual patrol, the king came across a woodcutter who was sitting by the roadside, weeping. The king approached him and asked, "Why are you crying, my good man?"

The woodcutter replied, "My king, I had trees in my orchard that I cut down to make coal and sell in the market. It supports my family. But now, all my trees are gone, and I have nothing left."

The king, moved by the man's plight, turned to his minister and instructed him to gift the woodcutter three new orchards so he could continue his work. The king felt a sense of happiness, knowing he had helped a man in need.

Several months passed, and during another one of his patrols, the king once again encountered the woodcutter – sitting in the same place, looking as miserable as before. The king was surprised and approached him. "What troubles you now?" the king asked.

The woodcutter sighed heavily and said, "My gracious king, I have exhausted my orchards once again. I cut down all the trees, made coal from them, and now I am again left with nothing."

The king was taken aback but remained silent for a moment. He then asked the woodcutter to follow him. They walked together until they reached one of the woodcutter's orchards where a small pile of wood was lying. The king picked up a piece and led the woodcutter to the market.

Once there, the king said, "My dear man, instead of turning this wood into coal, try selling it as it is." The woodcutter hesitated but did as the king **suggested**. To his astonishment, the wood sold for an incredibly high price.

The king's minister, who was accompanying them, revealed the truth. "The orchards that the king gifted you were filled with sandalwood trees," he explained. "Had you not burned them, you could have sold even a small portion and made much more than what you earned from coal."

What Do We Learn

Phokat mein barkat koni – there's no lasting blessing in something gained for free. The success that endures comes from what you build, not what you are given.

Often, businesses make the mistake of not recognising the true ingredients that drive long-term success. This is particularly relevant for businesses that depend too much on short-term gains, like grants or subsidies. While these external supports can help initiate or temporarily boost a business, they cannot sustain growth.

What's worse, this can also lead to a misalignment of priorities, with companies shifting their policies or strategies solely based on external support.

For example, in the case of green energy initiatives, many companies receive government grants to develop eco-friendly projects. While such incentives can spark development, they can also be misused; some businesses treat these grants as part of their regular cash flow, relying on them to cover operational costs rather than investing in long-term growth.

This short-sighted approach can create a dependency on subsidies, preventing companies from innovating or expanding sustainably. To address this concern, governments are increasingly attaching KPIs (key performance indicators) to ensure that these grants are used wisely and are directed towards areas that truly generate value.

A Window into My Experiences

In my journey, I have never depended on government grants or benefits to support my businesses. However, after analysing the stock market and various industries over the years, I have noticed that companies reliant on government incentives or bailouts tend to struggle **to create** long-term value.

In contrast, businesses that prioritise innovation, core growth, and the unique values of their ecosystem perform much better over time. I have seen this play out consistently, and I can confidently say that companies rooted in their own strengths have a far better track record. If you take a closer look at the stock market during the last twenty-five years, the trend becomes quite clear.

Now it's Your Turn!

Think of your business as an orchard. To yield a fruitful harvest, you must cultivate the soil, plant strong roots, and nurture your trees rather than waiting for fruits to drop into your lap. Here are some actionable steps:

1. **Plant the seeds of innovation:** Just as a farmer carefully selects seeds, focus on developing innovative products and services. Invest time in research and development to understand market needs, ensuring that your offerings are valuable and relevant.

2. **Use grants wisely:** If you receive grants or subsidies, think of them as fertiliser for your orchard. Use them strategically to invest in long-term projects that generate sustainable value rather than relying on them for daily expenses.

3. **Diversify your crops:** To minimise risk, diversify your revenue streams. Explore new markets, products, or services, and ensure that your business is not overly reliant on a single source of income.

***

Chapter 35

Ekk aur ekk do ko jod, saag saag gyaraah ko mol

(एक और एक दो को जोड़, साग साग ग्यारह को मोल)

A wise saying on the power of strategic partnerships in business

1 + 1 = 11?

In the world of business, success is rarely a solo effort. The magic truly happens when people come together, combining their strengths to create something far greater than they could on their own.

In other words, 1 + 1 = 11. The right teamwork does not just add; it multiplies.

Why this Multiplier Effect Works

The key to building a strong business partnership has always been the balance of skills. The (1 + 1 = 11) multiplier effect works because it is more than just adding people to a team; it is about creating a structure where individuals complement each other in a way that boosts everyone's potential. Whether in family businesses or broader partnerships, this collective energy drives greater productivity, innovation, and resilience.

But why is this particularly significant to the Marwaris? There is another facet to the story.

The Auspicious Nature of +1

In the Marwari tradition, numbers like 11, 21, 31, and 101 hold special value. The presence of one at the end is considered auspicious, symbolising new beginnings and a continuous cycle of growth. These numbers represent strength in unity.

In Marwari family businesses, this concept of synergy is even more pronounced. Brothers will divide their responsibilities based on their specific strengths. They work in harmony, combining their efforts to operate like a much larger team. Two brothers would function like eleven people, each contributing specialised skills to the whole.

Synergy in Skill Sets

Enter meaningful partnerships. Say, you are a businessperson with strong management skills. Your ideal partner would be someone with expertise in technology, creating a powerful combination. Similarly, if you are strong in product development but struggle with distribution, find a partner who excels in logistics. These partnerships have the potential to act as 11.

A Window into My Experiences

For me, having a great co-founder has always been a must, whether they are from within the family or outside of it. I value someone who has the courage to speak openly with me, and I make sure to have the courage to listen to their feedback. Communication cannot be a barrier between co-founders. When our skill sets complement each other, that is when we truly thrive as a team.

Now it's Your Turn!

The right partnerships and teamwork can transform a business. Here are some actionable steps you can take to harness this multiplier effect:

1. **Identify complementary skills:** Conduct a skillset analysis within your team to understand who excels in which areas. Tools like a skills matrix or SWOT analysis can help you match individuals with complementary abilities, ensuring a well-rounded and effective team.

2. **Form strategic partnerships:** Seek out external partners that fill the gaps in your business's capabilities. But approach these partnerships with a long-term mindset – do not just look for solutions to today's problems, but for those who will help you scale.

3. **Embrace family dynamics in business:** If you run a family business, embrace the tradition of leveraging family

members' unique strengths. Set boundaries between personal and business life to avoid conflicts and ensure each family member has a clear, defined role.

***

Chapter 36

Thare haath kaam, baki Ram ko naam

(थारे हाथ काम, बाकी राम को नाम)

A proverb about the importance of staying focused on your work, no matter the outcome

The Power of Faith and Trust in God

This age-old Marwari proverb captures the essence of how many Marwari businesspeople approach life and work. Let us explore it in detail.

Eye on Effort, Not Results

We touched upon this in one of our previous chapters as well. One of Bhagavad Gita's most well-known verses says, *"Karmanye vadhikaraste, ma phaleshu kadachana."*

Put simply, it asks us to give it our all but never be too attached to the result. Success or failure is not entirely up to us. There are larger forces at play, and the sooner we accept that the less stressful our journey becomes.

Why Lord Ram's Journey Matters

Marwaris often invoke the name of Lord Ram and for good reason. Ram's life was not smooth. He faced exile, separation from his wife Sita, and intense personal hardship. But even in the toughest times, he stayed focused on his duty and never lost faith. After all, it was Ram's endurance through challenges that transformed him from a prince into the God we worship today.

Lord Ram's story is a reminder that even the Gods face failure.

Do Not Let Failure Stop You – It is A Teacher

In business, failure is inevitable. It is part of the deal. The Marwaris embrace this fact; take a leaf out of their book. When you face setbacks – whether financial losses or personal struggles – do not lose courage. Instead, view the failures as opportunities to re-evaluate your strategy. Maybe it is time to change direction. Maybe you need to take a step back and look at the bigger picture.

Bounce Back with Faith

Just like Ram eventually conquered Ravan and brought Sita back, you too can overcome your challenges and bounce back stronger. Success may not come today or tomorrow, but if you keep moving forward, it will come.

Thare haath kaam – put in your best effort.

Baki Ram ko naam – But understand that the final outcome is not entirely in your hands. Some of it depends on destiny, or as they say, your faith in the divine.

A Window into My Experiences

I fully vouch for this *lokokti*. In business, perseverance is key. You have to keep going because after every night comes a new day. Business is not a smooth, paved road where you can just cruise in fourth gear – it is more of a rollercoaster. There will be highs and lows, good times and bad. Keep your faith in God, because while planning and capability matter, destiny plays its part too. You cannot control everything.

But do not lose hope when things slow down; use that time to prepare for what is ahead. And when the good times arrive, be quick to act and make the most of the opportunities. Success lies at the intersection of preparation and opportunity.

Now it's Your Turn!

There are countless external factors – economic downturns, shifting market trends, supply chain issues – that you simply cannot control. Here is what you can do instead:

1. **Take small steps every day:** Ensure your team is making daily progress, no matter how small. These incremental improvements build momentum over time.

2. **Plan for the long-term:** Develop both short-term and long-term strategies. Make sure you are not chasing quick wins at the expense of sustainable growth.

3. **Fail fast, learn faster:** If something is not working, recognise it early. Address issues head-on and move quickly to the next solution. The faster you learn from your mistakes, the faster you can adapt.

4. **Stay mission-driven:** Reaffirm your company's mission and values regularly. Keep the team aligned with the bigger picture, even during difficult times.

***

Chapter 37

Haare ka sahara Baba Shyam hamara, Balaji ko aasro, Jai Jeen Maata

(हारे का सहारा बाबा श्याम हमारा, बालाजी को आसरो, जय जीण माता)

———————❖———————

A generational mantra of faith and resilience

Three Divine Guides

Deeply rooted in the Marwari culture of Rajasthan's Shekhawati region, this chapter's proverb is a guiding principle for life and business. It is something that has been passed down through generations, keeping faith alive through every challenge, every success, and every tough decision.

Let us break it down, explore what it really means, and see how it influences the Marwari way of doing things.

Baba Shyam: The Protector When All Seems Lost

Haare ka sahara, Baba Shyam hamara – In defeat, Baba Shyam is our refuge

The first part of the *lokokti* centres on trusting Baba Shyam (Khatu Shyam *ji*), a beloved deity known for helping people in their darkest moments. The story behind Baba Shyam comes from the Mahabharata.

In Mahabharata, Barbarik, the grandson of Bheem, was an incredible warrior. He vowed to fight for the side that appeared to be losing. But when Lord Krishna realised Barbarik's unmatched strength could sway the outcome, he asked for Barbarik's head as a sacrifice. In return, Krishna blessed him, promising that he would be worshipped as Baba Shyam in *Kalyug*, helping those in need.

For Marwaris, this line invokes a divine reminder: no matter how tough things get, Baba Shyam is there. Whether it is a business setback or a personal challenge, there is always hope.

Balaji: The Ultimate Problem Solver

Balaji ko aasro – we seek refuge in Balaji

This second part refers to Lord Hanuman, or Balaji, who is often seen as the go-to deity when you are facing a big problem. The Salasar Balaji temple in Rajasthan is a major pilgrimage site where devotees come to pray for solutions to their troubles. It is like the spiritual equivalent of calling in the best troubleshooter you know when things start to go wrong.

Even in the Ramayana, Hanuman rescued Lakshman with the *Sanjeevani Booti*. For Marwari entrepreneurs, invoking Balaji's name gives them the strength and confidence to deal with business obstacles head-on.

Jai Jeen Maata: The Spirit of Celebration and Triumph

Jai Jeen Maata – Victory to the Divine Mother

The final part of the proverb calls upon Jeen Maata, a form of Devi Durga, the goddess of power and victory. Legend has it that even the mighty Mughal emperor Aurangzeb could not destroy her temple in Rajasthan.

In Marwari culture, Jai Jeen Maata is a reminder to celebrate victories – both big and small. Whether it is a business milestone or a personal achievement, this invocation of the Divine Mother signifies joy and strength.

Faith at the Core of Marwari Success

For centuries, the Marwari community has thrived in business. Ask them the secret, and along with hard work and sharp business acumen, they will tell you it is their faith. Likewise, the above *lokokti* is about knowing that even when things go wrong, divine support will help steer them through. That when things seem hopeless, the divine will step in to fight alongside them.

A Window into My Experiences

This proverb is deep-set in the Marwari business mind. First, it teaches you to deal with failures. Second, it instils the strength and hope you need to face challenges head-on. And third, it encourages you to celebrate every victory. This combination of faith, resilience, and celebration is what makes for a truly powerful formula in life and business.

Personally, I carry a photo of Balaji in my wallet wherever I go. It gives me a sense of conviction and belief that I am protected from all evils.

Now it's Your Turn!

This proverb can be your blueprint for success if used mindfully. Here are actionable steps that draw from this rich wisdom:

1. **Practise proactive problem-solving:** Encourage a culture where employees are empowered to address problems as they arise. Implement regular brainstorming sessions to identify potential issues before they escalate.

2. **Engage in community service:** Participate in community service projects that resonate with your company's values. This not only builds team spirit but also reinforces the idea of working towards a greater good.

***

Chapter 38

Ganesh biraje Riddhi Siddhi

(गणेश बिराजे रिद्धि सिद्धि)

A faith-driven saying on bringing prosperity to your business

The Lord of Wisdom at the Helm

Revered across India and beyond, Lord Ganesh stands as a symbol of wisdom, prosperity, and fresh beginnings. With His unique form adorned with symbols that represent intellect and success, Ganesh is the go-to God for the Marwaris, especially at the start of any new venture or project.

When you chant *Ganesh biraje Riddhi Siddhi*, you are inviting the Lord's presence into your life. But what does this saying *really* signify, and how does it relate to business? Let's take a closer look.

The Elephant-headed Harbinger of Fortune

Ganesh *ji's* unique form is not just visually striking; it also carries deep meanings. His large ears signify listening, while his small eyes represent focus – qualities that every entrepreneur needs when dealing with the ups and downs of business.

Biraje simply means to be present, so when you say it, you are praying to the Lord to guide you on your business journey.

Then there's Riddhi and Siddhi, Ganesh's two consorts. Riddhi symbolises wealth, not just money but the richness of knowledge, health, relationships, and more. Siddhi stands for success in all your efforts. Together, they signify that real success blends both material and spiritual wealth.

Balancing Wealth and Wisdom

Success requires a balance between material wealth and spiritual fulfilment. It is not about making more money; it is about growing as a person and learning continuously. And as you reach your goals, start giving back. Riddhi and Siddhi remind us of this generosity, encouraging us to share our blessings with others.

Ganesh *ji's* wisdom also tells us that success comes from working smart. So plan strategically before jumping into any new project. A solid plan lays the groundwork for growth.

Remember that there will be obstacles, but view them differently – not as roadblocks but as opportunities. Every challenge can be a stepping stone to something greater.

Lastly, build strong relationships. Do not just collect contacts; network meaningfully. Nurturing connections and growing together lead to mutual benefits. It is the relationships you build that help you grow in the long run.

A Window into My Experiences

Listening and reflection are essential ingredients of a robust leadership style. From my experience, the more I listen, the more wisdom and insight I gain. Taking time to reflect helps me think about moving forward while staying focused.

Marwari businesspeople seek both solace and solutions in Ganesh *ji's* wisdom.

Now it's Your Turn!

The mantra of *Ganesh biraje Riddhi Siddhi* is more than just a call to seek blessings. Here are some practical steps for your business inspired by this mantra:

1. **Build a solid base:** Hold quarterly strategy meetings to review your business plan and make updates as needed.

2. **Connect and grow your network:** Go to industry events, trade shows, and local business gatherings to meet new people. Stay in touch with them to strengthen the relationships.

3. **Define goals and celebrate wins:** Set up a success board for the team to showcase achievements and plan monthly celebrations to recognise milestones.

***

Chapter 39

Lakshmi ko vas

(लक्ष्मी को वास)

*A wise saying on creating a safe and ethical space
for your business*

The House of the Goddess

Goddess Lakshmi, the symbol of prosperity, settles where there is integrity, good deeds, and respect. For modern businesses, that means building environments where everyone feels valued and safe – no exceptions. So, how do you invite that kind of lasting success into your business? Let's understand.

Start with Integrity

Integrity is not just good for the soul; it is also good for your business. After all, it is the foundation of trust. When you are straightforward with your employees, customers, and partners, people notice, and that builds real loyalty.

People want to work for, buy from, and support businesses they believe in. So, by staying true to your word and keeping your actions transparent, you can create a place where trust naturally flourishes – and with it, long-term success.

Next, Address Inclusion

You should view inclusion as more than just a 'policy'. Creating a genuinely inclusive environment means everyone has a voice and feels welcome. When you commit to actively removing barriers – whether that is addressing gender bias or providing equal opportunities – you are building a foundation where everyone can contribute their best. And the benefits are real: businesses that prioritise inclusion tend to be more innovative, resilient, and ready to adapt.

Put simply: Lakshmi thrives in places that celebrate every individual's potential.

Finally, Build a Legacy Beyond Profit

A business built on respect, fairness, and integrity leaves a legacy that outlasts any quarterly gains.

This kind of legacy is powerful. It inspires others to do better, be better, and support something they believe in. But that reputation is not built overnight; it is earned over years of aligning actions with values, of standing firm on principles even when it is tough.

In this way, the spirit of *Lakshmi ko vas* lives on.

A Window into My Experiences

When I think about any workplace, I believe the most important thing is to cultivate an environment grounded in purity. For me, this has always meant creating spaces where everyone feels valued, safe and free from the negative effects of individual politics.

I have always strived to build open communication so that team members can express their thoughts and ideas without hesitation. It is important that everyone upholds integrity and ethical practices, avoiding any wrongful deeds that could compromise trust.

I see our team not just as colleagues but as a community working together towards shared goals, ultimately leading to greater satisfaction and success for all of us.

Now it's Your Turn!

True prosperity flourishes where respect and good deeds are prioritised. Here are some actionable steps to turn this vision into reality.

- **Foster an inclusive culture beyond diversity and inclusion policies:** Go beyond diversity quotas by fostering genuine inclusivity – offer training on unconscious bias, create platforms for employees to voice ideas and review policies to remove any barriers to inclusion.

- **Take a stand against discrimination, including sexual harassment:** Develop and enforce strong anti-discrimination and anti-harassment policies. Train managers on recognising and addressing inappropriate behaviour, and create a safe channel for reporting issues.

- **Support employee growth and fair opportunities:** Offer equal training, development, and advancement opportunities to all employees, ensuring promotions and rewards are based on performance, not bias. Introduce mentorship programmes to support career growth across all levels.

***

Chapter 40

Be-mausam ki barsaat mein upaaj koni

(बे-मौसम की बरसात में उपज कोनी)

* * *

A lesson about patience and timing in business

In Untimely Rains, There is No Harvest

Ever tried planting a garden only to have a sudden rainstorm wash away your hopes? That is the essence of this *lokokti*. This proverb teaches us a valuable lesson: trying to grow something when conditions are not right is often a waste of effort. Understanding when to push forward and when to step back can make all the difference in your journey.

The Impact of Tailwinds and Headwinds

Think of tailwinds and headwinds as the forces that shape your business path. Tailwinds are those moments when everything seems to fall into place, propelling you towards your goals. Whether it is a surge in market demand or a well-timed opportunity, these favourable conditions can make your work feel effortless.

On the other hand, headwinds represent challenges that slow you down – economic downturns, fierce competition, or unexpected setbacks.

When you experience a tailwind, seize the opportunity. But do not become complacent; there might be potential headwinds ahead. Anticipating challenges helps you strategise effectively and remain resilient.

The Mango Metaphor

Did you know, mangoes are the perfect metaphor for growth? Just like the fruit thrives only in its specific season, your business needs the right timing and environment to flourish. You need to respect the natural rhythm of growth.

However, this does not mean that you should be passive; it means that you should be proactive about your timing. Look for indicators that signal when it is the right moment to take action.

Nurturing Growth is All About Intentionality

Regularly assess the progress of your projects and be open to adjusting your approach based on what you observe. Are your efforts bearing fruit, or do they need a little more time and care?

Consider integrating feedback loops into your process. This could mean soliciting input from your team, customers, or stakeholders to understand what is working and what is not. That way, you not only react to external conditions but also proactively shape the growth of your initiatives.

Stay Adaptable Along the Way

Recognise that sometimes, taking a break can be just as important as pushing forward. If you find yourself facing persistent headwinds, consider pausing to regroup. This pause can provide clarity, helping you reassess your goals and refine your strategies without the pressure of constant forward motion.

When the going gets tough, reach out to your network for support and collaboration. Building a community around your initiatives provides a safety net and also opens up new perspectives.

And Finally, Trust the Process

Patience is your best ally. Sustainable success comes from giving yourself the grace to grow at your own pace.

When you find yourself feeling impatient, remind yourself of the natural cycles of life. Just like the seasons change, your efforts will eventually yield results. Focus on the small wins along the way and celebrate the progress you make, even if it feels slow.

A Window into My Experiences

Success, I will reiterate, is where opportunity meets preparation. It is a delicate balance, and I have learnt that both elements are equally important.

Persistence hence plays a crucial role, much like driving on a highway. There are times when the road is bumpy, and that is when you should slow down and navigate carefully. But then there are those clear days when the weather is perfect and the road ahead is unobstructed. In those moments, shift into fourth gear and accelerate towards your goals.

Now it's Your Turn!

Growth flourishes in the right conditions. Here are some actionable steps to help you get started:

- **Adapt your strategies:** When faced with challenges, assess your strategies and be ready to pivot. This might involve modifying product offerings, adjusting marketing approaches, or exploring new markets. Using agile project management practices can help you maintain flexibility throughout this process.

- **Leverage feedback and insights:** Establish systems to gather customer feedback on your products or services. Hold regular team retrospectives to discuss successes and challenges, building a collaborative environment for innovative ideas and strategies.

***

Chapter 41

Kumkum, tikko, akshat laage

(कुमकुम, टिक्को, अक्षत लागे)

———❖———

*A timeless saying on the essence of blessings and
purity in our lives*

More Than a Mark

In Marwari culture, applying *tikko* with *kumkum* and *akshat* is a celebration of life's milestones. It sets the tone for new beginnings, whether in life or business. So, let's explore this tradition and understand how you can channel its wisdom into your own endeavours.

Understanding the Symbolism

Let's start with the basics: *kumkum* is a vibrant red powder, often placed on the forehead, symbolising auspiciousness. *Akshat*, on the other hand, is made from unbroken rice grains, representing prosperity and abundance. Together, they create a blessing that

199

protects and promotes success. So, when you apply a marking on your forehead with *kumkum* and *akshat*, you follow a tradition that infuses your projects with positive intentions.

Now, think about your own business ventures. What if you approached each new project with the same mindset?

The Strength of a Solid Foundation

Just like laying a solid base for a building, applying *kumkum* symbolises the start of good things. It sets a positive tone and signals readiness for new beginnings in your business.

This foundation is strengthened by embracing gratitude along the journey. Acknowledging the blessings you receive, from supportive mentors to dedicated team members, creates an uplifting atmosphere for growth. Fostering a culture of appreciation elevates your own spirit and inspires those around you to flourish.

The Power of Pure Integrity

As you cultivate gratitude, do not overlook the importance of integrity. This value plays a vital role in the symbolism of *akshat*. Just as *akshat* signifies purity, your business practices should reflect honesty and ethical values. A reputation based on integrity attracts opportunities and fosters trust among clients and partners. Regularly assess your operations to ensure transparency and fairness, laying a solid foundation for long-term success.

Build Meaningful Relationships Along the Way

The application of *kumkum* and *akshat* underlines the spirit of community and connection in both personal and professional realms. Networking becomes essential; just as families unite during rituals, make an effort to connect with like-minded professionals in your industry. Attend events, engage in discussions, and explore collaborative opportunities that resonate with your values.

A Window into My Experiences

I will reiterate when I reflect on the remarkable rise of certain communities in business, particularly those from Rajasthan and Haryana, it is fascinating to consider what really drives their success.

One big piece of the puzzle is the practice of applying *tikko*. It is more than a ritual; it is like laying down a solid foundation for everything that comes next. When Marwaris put that *tikko* on their foreheads, it signals that they are ready for new beginnings and good things ahead.

But there is more to it. *Akshat* represents consistency and purity in intentions. This kind of consistency builds deep confidence that stems from knowing that you have the right intentions – almost like having a blessing from above. It empowers the Marwaris to pursue their goals without fear.

So, for these communities, *tikko* and *akshat* become more than tradition. They become a way of life that shapes how they do business. It creates a positive mindset where each new venture is approached with excitement and purpose, leading to a vibrant business culture that others look up to.

Now it's Your Turn!

Much like the traditions of *kumkum, tikko, akshat laage* that celebrate milestones and community, creating an environment where every member feels valued can lead to remarkable outcomes. Here are some actionable steps to help you channel that spirit:

- **Cultivate a culture of gratitude:** Celebrate team achievements. Whether through monthly meetings or a simple thank you email, make it a point to recognise contributions. Additionally, create a feedback system that encourages open communication, mirroring the communal spirit celebrated during rituals.

- **Encourage collaboration over competition:** Form teams composed of members from different departments to tackle specific projects or challenges. This encourages diverse perspectives and innovative solutions.

***

Chapter 42

Garje jeeko, barse koni
(गरजै जिको, बरसै कोनी)

A wise saying on the power of actions over words

Promises Don't Rain

The proverb literally translates to 'The clouds that thunder the most, rain the least'. In essence, you should let your actions do the talking. Because promises do not bring results – real action does.

In business, we have all seen the difference between someone who makes big promises and someone who actually delivers. This wisdom teaches us to keep things real, focus on what we do rather than what we say, and, in the process, build a strong reputation.

Show, Don't Tell

If you constantly promise big results but do not deliver, it is only a matter of time before people start doubting you. Rather than relying on bold statements, let your work create your reputation.

Consistency speaks volumes, and when your actions back up your claims, you create a track record people trust. It is this steady reliability that clients, partners, and employees respect – and keep coming back for.

Create Value Without the Show

Meaningful actions are about delivering value, even when nobody's watching. Rather than aiming for showy announcements, focus on incremental improvements. Quietly invest time and energy into improving your product or service, listening to feedback, and doing the little things that make a big difference in the long run.

People notice genuine effort and value – it is a quiet strength that is much louder than any marketing pitch. This approach speaks to the heart of *garje jeeko, barse koni* – focusing on value over hype.

A Window into My Experiences

My experience has taught me that when you make a bold statement, you must back it up with action. Similarly, when you promote a product or service, it is essential to deliver messages that genuinely reflect what you offer. If your ads promise results without delivering, you risk damaging your credibility, which is challenging to rebuild once lost.

Effective communication involves more than just shouting your message; it requires creating a meaningful dialogue with your audience. As you build your credibility through honest advertising, you will find that even a small amount of communication can yield significant results. When your audience trusts your brand, they are more likely to engage, convert, and become loyal customers.

Remember, in advertising, substance always outweighs style.

Now it's Your Turn!

Build a resilient business admired for its matter rather than its noise. Here are some actionable steps:

- **Build a culture of results, not promises:** At the start of each project, clearly define what success looks like in measurable terms. Conduct monthly reviews to ensure your actions are on track with these goals. Track this in a visible place, like a shared team dashboard, to encourage a results-driven mindset.

- **Grow authentic partnerships, not showy collaborations:** When choosing a partner, set criteria that go beyond marketing potential. Measure the partnership's impact through actual results – whether that's in customer satisfaction, improved processes, or increased innovation – rather than immediate visibility.

- **Communicate results only when they are concrete:** For new product launches or service expansions, hold back from making announcements until you have achieved clear, demonstrable success. When ready, communicate this through a case study, sharing not only the result but also the journey of how you got there, which builds deeper trust.

***

- **Communicate results only when they are concrete:** For new product launches or service expansions, hold back from making announcements until you have achieved clear, demonstrable success. When ready, communicate this through a case study, sharing not only the result but also the journey of how you got there, which builds deeper trust.

Chapter 43

Ghora ki chaal, sidhi hi chokhi

(घोड़ा की चाल, सीधी ही चौखी)

*A timeless saying on maintaining laser
focus in business*

Have You Seen a Horse Running Haywire Win a Race?

Unlikely. The horse's stride is best when it is straight. And that is exactly the wisdom the *lokokti* of this chapter has to offer.

Just like a horse galloping in a clear direction, a business that avoids distractions is primed for success. But focus is not about being rigid – it is about knowing when to stay the course and when to adapt.

Eyes on the Big Picture

Business is full of distractions – new trends, competitor moves, and unexpected challenges. Long-term success, however, is rooted in staying true to your mission. When you know exactly where you are headed, it is much easier to cut through the noise and focus on what truly matters.

But Do Not Ignore the World

While focus is essential, staying aware of your surroundings cannot be overlooked. Market changes, shifting customer needs, and competitor moves are all worth paying attention to.

It is a balance. A horse is not distracted by every blade of grass on its path; it stays focused on the finish line. Your business, too, needs that single-mindedness to drive meaningful results. But staying aware helps you pivot smartly when necessary.

Think in the Long-Term

Sustainable growth is built on patience. Keep a steady pace and an eye on the horizon. Short-term wins can be exciting, but they should not come at the cost of your long-term stability. Success often comes down to sticking with your vision and building on it year after year.

Recognise the Cost of Distraction

A lack of focus can lead to overextended resources and energy drained in too many directions. It is easy to feel like you are accomplishing more by juggling multiple initiatives, but often, this approach dilutes your impact. True productivity comes from investing deeply in fewer, more strategic areas.

A Window into My Experiences

Focus is one of the most valuable lessons I have learnt in both my personal and professional life. Distractions can lead to costly mistakes in a startup environment, but that does not mean you should avoid experimentation. Start with ten ideas, then narrow it down to three. Once you have identified those three, let go of the rest and concentrate on them until you can further refine your focus to just one.

While it is easy to advocate for focus, determining where to direct that focus can be quite challenging. Your experiences and experiments will guide you in making those decisions. Flexibility and adaptability are key in this process.

Now it's Your Turn!

Here are some actionable steps to turn the *lokokti's* focus into your practice:

- **Define clear, long-term goals:** Start by establishing your business's primary objectives for the next few years. Use quarterly reviews to ensure that day-to-day actions align with these goals.

- **Prioritise tasks to maintain focus:** Categorise tasks by urgency and impact. Use tools like the Eisenhower Matrix to focus on high-impact, high-priority work. Delegate or minimise time on low-priority tasks to prevent noise from derailing your focus.

- **Invest in fewer, high-impact projects:** Choose one or two key initiatives that align with your core objectives. Fully commit resources to ensure these projects are successful before branching out to new ventures.

- **Monitor and minimise distractions:** Identify and limit time on tasks that do not directly support your goals. Consider designating specific time blocks for emails, social media, or unplanned meetings to avoid constant interruptions.

***

Chapter 44

Pagdi ki izzat

(पगड़ी की इज़्ज़त)

———※※———

A proverb that signifies the importance of upholding one's honour and reputation

The Pride of the Marwari Tradition

In Marwari culture, the *pagdi* (turban) is far more than a headpiece; it is a symbol of dignity, respect, and a reflection of deep-rooted values. It carries the pride of generations and is a visible reminder of the family honour that each Marwari holds dear.

Let's explore the multiple roles it plays at the core of the community.

A Marker of Dignity and Responsibility

The *pagdi* carries immense significance. It embodies the responsibilities, values, and ethics passed down from elders. Marwari parents and grandparents often remind younger generations to uphold the *pagdi ki izzat* – a gentle nudge to stay rooted in tradition, act with integrity, and make choices that respect the family legacy.

For them, honour is not something you buy; it is something you build, protect, and pass on. Success might come and go, but your *pagdi*, your honour, should remain spotless.

A Legacy of Values

The *pagdi* is also seen as a form of inheritance – not in terms of money or property, but in the values it represents. When a Marwari father ties the *pagdi* on his son's head at ceremonies, it is a meaningful gesture that says, "This is your responsibility now; uphold our name and our values."

In Marwari business culture, this sense of honour takes on even greater importance. A Marwari's word is as binding as a contract, which is why handshake deals remain a hallmark of their business dealings. Every promise and decision reflects on the family's honour, woven tightly with the values of the *pagdi*.

Pagdi and the Community

The *pagdi* also plays a key role in uniting the Marwari community. In gatherings, you would see distinctive turbans worn by elders as a mark of their standing and respect within the community. Meanwhile, the younger generation learns early on that their actions contribute to the collective honour.

Pagdi and *Bhamashahs*

This proverb will not be complete if I don't mention the *Bhamashahs*.

A special place in Marwari culture is reserved for the *Bhamashahs* – individuals who give back generously to the community, be it through philanthropy, supporting education, or uplifting local causes. In ceremonies, *pagdis* are presented to them as a gesture of public recognition and gratitude.

This tradition not only celebrates individual contributions but also inspires others to step up and serve the community.

A Window into My Experiences

I mentioned earlier in a previous chapter how Marwari businesspeople place immense importance on the *rukka* (an informal promissory note). As a professional, I have witnessed this firsthand since my early days in Kolkata. A *rukka* is always honoured, no matter the circumstances. It is this unwavering commitment to keeping one's word that has been the bedrock of trust within the community and a key factor in its growth and success.

And this essence of mutual trust and honour ties back to the overarching *pagdi ki izzat,* the importance of honouring every promise, whether in business or life.

While modern tools like emails, digital contracts, and other formal mechanisms are indispensable for large organisations, the dynamics of small to medium-sized enterprises (true for many Marwari businesses) are often rooted in a different ethos. In these settings, trust is paramount. So, a verbal agreement or a handwritten *rukka* often holds greater significance and reliability than even a cheque.

Now it's Your Turn!

Use the wisdom of *pagdi ki izzat* as a practical guide to build a business that grows sustainably, fosters respect, and leaves a lasting, honourable legacy in the marketplace. Here are some actionable steps:

1. **Develop a 'handshake culture' of trust:** Encourage a company culture where a commitment, even if verbal, is honoured fully. This could mean documenting commitments transparently and promptly fulfilling obligations without delay.

2. **Create a legacy of accountability:** As a leader, act as a role model. When mistakes happen, take responsibility rather than deflecting blame. Encourage accountability across all levels and recognise employees who demonstrate commitment to the company's values.

3. **Build a respectful above-profit mindset:** Train your team to focus on ethical sales, avoiding high-pressure tactics or promises that cannot be met. Celebrate wins achieved with integrity and publicly recognise employees who make values-driven choices.

***

Chapter 45

Dudh mein misri ki jiya ghul jaano

(दूध में मिसरी की जिया घुल जाणौ)

A wise saying that highlights the art of blending in gracefully

Melt like Sugar in Milk

The *lokokti* of this chapter literally translates to the above. It is a beautiful way to describe a personality that easily blends into its surroundings with grace, just as sugar dissolves into milk without creating a stir, only adding sweetness.

In Marwari culture, this proverb represents an ideal way of being – gentle, kind-hearted, and bringing harmony wherever one goes.

Gentleness is a Strength

The community values strength, but not the kind that is loud or overbearing. Rather, it is the quiet strength that comes from a gentle heart and a humble attitude. To *melt like sugar in milk* is to bring warmth and kindness into every interaction, blending effortlessly without drawing attention.

In Marwari households, children are taught to be gentle and considerate, showing respect to both family members and guests. This approach is not just something that applies at home; it carries over into business and personal relationships. The belief is simple: kindness wins hearts, builds lasting connections, and creates strong alliances.

This way of adding value is understated, almost natural. It is a quiet form of generosity, where giving is done without any expectation of recognition.

A Sweet Disposition as a Bridge in Business and Community

Marwaris often see a sweet, calm disposition as a key to success, especially in business. *Dudh mein misri ki jiya ghul jaano* encourages them to approach clients, customers, and even competitors with politeness and patience, creating a foundation of mutual respect and trust. For Marwari businesspeople, a warm, respectful demeanour is often as essential as their natural business acumen.

This mindset has contributed to their business success across generations.

Blending into New Communities

Marwaris also have a long history of migration, moving from their homeland to places like Kolkata, Mumbai, Chennai, and even abroad to the U.S., U.K., and Africa. Wherever they go, they are known for their ability to respect local traditions, learn the local language, and adapt to the local way of life.

For instance, Marwaris in Kolkata often speak fluent Bengali and participate in local festivals like Durga Puja, while those in Tamil Nadu might celebrate Pongal with their Tamil neighbours. At the same time, they continue to celebrate Marwari festivals, teach their children their customs, and preserve their cultural practices, bridging the gap between their heritage and their new home.

Integrating into Business Environments

Wherever Marwaris establish businesses – whether in Gujarat's textile markets, Mumbai's finance hubs or Delhi's trade centres – they skilfully adapt to local business practices, etiquettes and customs. This flexibility makes them reliable and relatable partners in the business world. They show deep respect for the regional norms and methods while bringing their own core values of trust, humility, and quiet resilience into the mix.

A Window into My Experiences

I am originally from Rajasthan (and now settled in Kolkata) and have a lot of friends in the Bengali community. I have also had the chance to visit Mumbai, and what always stands out to me is the way Marwaris have adapted so respectfully in both places.

They treat the land as their own, continue their entrepreneurial journey, and remain deeply involved in the local community. They blend business with philanthropy, always giving back through their active participation. In both Kolkata and Mumbai, I have never witnessed any resistance from the locals. Instead, the Marwaris have been welcomed with open arms and have settled in peacefully.

There is also a great cultural exchange between the communities. Some of my Bengali friends have learnt the art of doing business from the Marwaris, while the Marwaris have learnt art and music from the Bengalis, who are experts in these fields. It is a beautiful give-and-take that enriches both sides, and it shows how Marwaris can integrate seamlessly wherever they go.

Now it's Your Turn!

Just like sugar melts into milk without disrupting its essence, successful businesses blend into new markets with respect and humility. Here are some actionable steps to help you:

1. **Adapt to local business practices:** If you are opening a new branch in a different region or country, learn about the local business etiquette, whether it is how deals are made, communication styles, or the preferred way to address customers and partners. Tailoring your approach to these local norms shows respect and helps you integrate smoothly.

2. **Use soft power to strengthen your brand:** Make sure your marketing messages reflect your commitment to quality, ethical practices, and customer-first values. Encourage customers to share their positive experiences, but let the feedback come naturally, rather than forcing or overselling.

3. **Focus on quiet excellence:** Strive to deliver exceptional customer service and quality. Rather than advertising every small win, make a habit of consistently exceeding customer expectations. Over time, this builds a strong reputation for reliability and excellence.

***

Chapter 46

Chokho muhurat, Riddhi Siddhi, subh labh Ganesh ki gaddi

(चौखो मुहूरत, रिद्धि सिद्धि, शुभ लाभ गणेश की गद्दी)

A timeless wisdom highlighting the importance of starting right

The Marwari Way to Auspiciousness

In Marwari culture, auspicious beginnings and divine blessings are seen as integral to success. This chapter's proverb combines these elements beautifully, linking the notion of starting anything significant at an auspicious time (*chokho muhurat*) with the blessings of Lord Ganesh, the remover of obstacles and harbinger of success, prosperity, and well-being.

Chokho Muhurat: the Power of Timing

For Marwaris, timing is key. The idea of starting something important at an auspicious time (*chokho muhurat*) is deeply rooted in their culture. It is believed that the right timing aligns your actions with the cosmic energies, ensuring the best possible outcome.

Whether it is starting a new business, making a significant investment, or embarking on a personal journey, Marwaris consult religious calendars and seek advice from elders to ensure that they begin their ventures at the most favourable time. It is not just about luck; it is about creating harmony with the universe right from the start.

Riddhi Siddhi: Seeking Blessings for Success

Riddhi and *Siddhi* represent the blessings of wealth and wisdom (Ganesh *ji's* two consorts). Marwari entrepreneurs are often seen invoking Ganesh *ji's* blessings before opening their shops, starting new projects or entering into new business deals. This reflects the deep belief in the power of knowledge and divine grace to steer them through challenges.

Subh Labh Ganesh ki Gaddi: Inviting Prosperity and Good Fortune

Prosperity (*subh*) and good fortune (*labh*) are believed to reside on the throne of Lord Ganesh (*Ganesh ki gaddi*). When embarking on important milestones, it is common for Marwaris to place an idol of Lord Ganesh in their homes or workplaces as a way to invite prosperity and ensure a positive start.

But at the same time, they combine these spiritual practices with modern business strategies, equipping themselves with up-to-date market insights, digital tools, and strategic plans. In this way, Marwaris blend faith with practical action, creating a foundation for both material success and cultural fulfilment.

A Window into My Experiences

Let me share an honest confession here: when I was preparing to start my own business, tradition suggested I begin at an auspicious *muhurat*. But my scientific mindset told me it did not matter; I could start whenever. My father insisted on waiting for the right moment as well, but honestly, it still did not excite me much. I did not see the point in delaying something I was so eager to begin.

But as I got older, I began reading the Upanishads. I realised how these seemingly small things could actually energise the mind. Starting at a specific time with a particular focus can really make a difference.

I also learnt about the significance of the first Ganesh Puja. Ganesh *ji's* large ears, which symbolise listening more carefully, made me reflect on how starting after His puja could help me focus more on my business growth.

Today, I realise that whether it is science or not, there is definitely something about starting at a particular time that creates a sense of excitement. When your family and friends come together to celebrate and wish you luck at the start of a venture, you naturally feel more energised and confident.

And this is especially true for entrepreneurs.

Because entrepreneurship is not just about action; it is also about imagination. And when that imagination is fuelled by excitement, it is a double win. It gives you the confidence that you have started at the right time and that psychological boost makes a big difference.

Now it's Your Turn!

With the blessings of Lord Ganesh, here's how you can infuse the *lokokti's* wisdom in your business practices:

1. **Start at the right time:** Consult with advisers or conduct research to choose an optimal time to make major moves, such as launching a product or expanding your business. Involve your team in decision-making to ensure alignment and collective buy-in.

2. **Seek blessings for wisdom and success:** Consider starting a team ritual or moment of reflection for key milestones (e.g., a brief prayer or meditation session) to set a positive tone for the journey ahead. This practice creates a sense of purpose and unity within your team.

3. **Combine spirituality and strategy:** Alongside spiritual practices, invest in market research, digital tools, and financial strategies that ensure success. Make data-driven decisions while keeping the human element in mind – whether it is customer relations, product quality, or team morale.

***

Chapter 47

Moli ko mol koni

(मोली को मोल कोनी)

*A proverb on the immeasurable value of trust, blessings,
and ethical responsibility*

Have You Ever Noticed Marwaris Wearing a Thread Around Their Wrists?

It is called *moli*.

This chapter's proverb is a statement, not about the thread's monetary value but about its emotional, cultural, and symbolic significance. For Marwaris, the *moli* represents faith, trust, and the continuity of traditions.

Let's take a closer look.

Why Moli Matters?

The *moli*, a sacred red and yellow thread, is tied during rituals and prayers, signifying divine blessings and protection. It acts as a constant, tangible reminder of commitments – spiritual, familial, or even professional.

In Marwari households, the act of tying a *moli* is also a moment of grounding. Whether it is during Ganesh Puja or a business inauguration, the thread symbolises starting something new with intention, focus, and a sense of responsibility.

Starting a new venture with the blessings of elders, symbolised by tying a *moli*, creates a psychological edge. It instils confidence and a sense of purpose, reminding entrepreneurs of their roots while they take bold steps forward.

The Unseen Value in Business and Life

Moli ko mol koni is a lesson in recognising and respecting the intangible. Whether in life or business, not everything valuable can be measured in monetary terms. The *moli* stands for trust, blessings, and the quiet strength of tradition. It is invaluable.

For Marwari entrepreneurs, it acts as a metaphor for how they approach challenges: with humility, focus, and a grounding in their values.

So the next time you see a *moli*, think of it as more than a thread. It is a symbol of promises kept, values upheld, and blessings carried forward – a priceless legacy woven into everyday life and business.

A Window into My Experiences

From my childhood to this day, I have never gone a single day without a *moli* tied around my wrist. There were times when I wondered if it truly made a difference or if it was just psychological. But as I grew older and entered the world of business, I realised how much self-confidence can the simple *moli* induce, especially during critical meetings or when dealing with difficult clients. In those moments, you often need a spiritual boost, something to steady your mind and strengthen your resolve.

Whenever I extend my right hand for a handshake with stakeholders, the *moli* always catches my attention first. It feels like an unseen transmission of energy from my hand to my mind, a quick reminder that I am protected and blessed. It grounds me with a sense of purpose and security.

It is much like oxygen in life; you do not consciously value it every moment, yet it is absolutely essential. Or like the sun, whose presence we often take for granted but is vital for existence. The *moli*, a simple cotton thread dyed in the natural colours of red and yellow, holds similar significance. It symbolises protection and strength, bringing confidence to the mind, which in turn leads to better and more successful business decisions.

Now it's Your Turn!

The *moli* might be a small, simple thread, but it carries with it the weight of tradition and the power of belief. Here are some actionable steps you can take to instil its wisdom:

- **Start every project with intention and focus:** Before launching a project or initiative, take a moment to define clear goals and intentions. Conduct a small inaugural ceremony or gathering to mark the beginning and set the tone for success.

- **Use symbolism to energise your team:** Celebrate milestones with simple but meaningful gestures, like appreciation notes or small gatherings. Create rituals that signify unity and shared purpose, such as team brainstorming sessions before launching major projects.

- **Recognise the value of intangibles:** Regularly invest in strengthening your reputation through excellent customer service, ethical practices, and consistent quality. Celebrate intangible successes like customer satisfaction and employee happiness alongside financial milestones.

***

Chapter 48

Gamcho aur loto hi toh laya tha

(गमछो और लोटो ही तो लाया था)

A proverb on the seed of a risk-taking mindset

An Ode to Humble Beginnings

This proverb speaks volumes about the resilience and risk-taking mindset of the Marwari community, especially during their early days of migration. Let's explore what it really means and how it shaped the entrepreneurial spirit that drives so many Marwari businesses today.

The Journey of Migration: From Rajasthan to New Horizons

For generations, the Marwari community has been known for its entrepreneurial prowess, but their journey started with humble beginnings. Many Marwaris, as they migrated from their homeland in Rajasthan, Haryana, and Malwa, arrived in new territories with little more than their basic belongings – a *gamcho* (a simple cotton towel) and a *loto* (a small water vessel used for daily tasks). They came with almost nothing, but they brought with them something far more valuable: an unshakable will to succeed.

This proverb highlights the simplicity of their beginnings.

Risk-taking: The Core of Marwari Entrepreneurship

The proverb also reflects the Marwaris' fearless approach to risk. With nothing substantial to lose except for a towel and a water vessel, the community viewed their challenges with a unique perspective. When you start with little or nothing, the fear of loss does not hold you back. You have nothing to lose, so you take risks without hesitation.

In fact, this mindset became the seed of the Marwari risk-taking mentality. Marwaris have always been willing to step into uncharted territories, launch new businesses, or make investments in unfamiliar areas – because, at their core, they understood that the potential for growth outweighed the risk of failure.

But Marwaris are Not Reckless in Their Approach

The key part of this mindset is the ability to measure what is at stake. Yes, the maximum they could lose was their *gamcho* and *loto*, but they still approached every new venture with meticulous planning, focus, and dedication.

Before taking any significant steps, they would weigh the risks and rewards, ensuring that their decisions were made with a clear understanding of what they stood to gain and what they could afford to lose. This level of pragmatism and clarity is what enabled them to take bold steps with confidence.

A Window into My Experiences

When starting any business, there is an unspoken reality: out of ten initiatives, if even three succeed, you have the potential to become a multi-millionaire. But that also means that 70% of your efforts are likely to fail. And there is no way of knowing the order in which success and failure will come.

The key, then, is resilience. After experiencing failures, financial losses, and setbacks, how do you maintain the confidence to try again? How do you absorb the loss, manage the disappointment, and keep moving forward? This is where the essence of the proverb comes into play.

In Rajasthan, there is a common saying when reflecting on hardships: "When we came from our village, we had nothing. Whatever we have built, we built with our own hands. Whatever we lose, we lose here, not from our community or our home." This perspective builds courage and acceptance of the inevitable highs and lows of business. Profit and loss are part of the journey.

The wisdom here lies in recognising that you started with nothing but your determination and effort. So, even if you lose what you have earned, you have not lost your ability to rebuild. This mindset helps Marwari entrepreneurs take calculated risks, absorb setbacks, and keep striving for success.

Now it's Your Turn!

Today, the Marwari approach to risk has evolved but still retains its core principles. The modern Marwari entrepreneur embraces risk but with a balanced approach. Here's how you can do it too:

1. **Start with what you have:** Assess the resources you currently have, however limited. Often, we wait for the perfect moment or the ideal resources to start. Instead, begin with what is available – your skills, ideas, and a basic plan. Create a minimum viable product (MVP) or service to test the waters. Start small, gather feedback, and iterate.

2. **Embrace calculated risk-taking:** Risk is inherent in entrepreneurship, but it is essential to take calculated risks. Before making decisions, assess what is at stake. How much can you afford to lose? What is the potential upside? Use tools like SWOT analysis to evaluate your business opportunities before jumping in.

3. **Measure what is at stake:** While it is important to take risks, be mindful of what you stand to lose – especially in terms of reputation, relationships, and resources. Starting small reduces the exposure to big risks, making it easier to bounce back if things do not go as planned. Think about the worst-case scenario and how you can minimise potential losses. For instance, if you are launching a new product, consider a small-scale test market first to gauge customer response.

***

Chapter 49

Bhagwan ki paanti sab se sacchi

(भगवान की पांति सब से सच्ची)

A timeless saying on divine support and belief

Have You Ever Considered Making God Your Business Partner?

In the Marwari community, there is a deeply ingrained belief in making God a partner in one's business. This chapter's proverb reflects this philosophy – essentially, it suggests that having God as a partner ensures honesty, ethical practices, and a sense of divine protection in every venture.

Let's break down this concept and understand how it shapes business as well as influences personal values and philanthropic practices.

God as a Business Partner

In many Marwari businesses, a portion of the profits is automatically set aside for charity or to support religious institutions like Salasar Balaji, Baba Shyam, or a personal charitable trust. This practice reflects the belief that involving God in your business dealings creates a sense of accountability and trustworthiness.

Divine Support for Success and Challenges

Divine presence then becomes a stabilising force. Whether the business faces a windfall or a downturn, God's partnership ensures that the entrepreneur's efforts are always supported and the rewards are just. This strengthens the belief that both success and failure are part of a larger cosmic plan and that the ultimate goal is not just profit, but a sense of righteousness and responsibility.

Philanthropy on Autopilot

One of the most beautiful aspects of this belief system is that it makes philanthropic contributions automatic, happening without extra effort or thought. The practice of setting aside a percentage of profits for God or charitable causes ensures that giving back becomes part of the routine, rather than an afterthought. Over time, this practice creates a sustainable flow of support to the community and the less fortunate, without requiring additional planning or decision-making.

Ethical and Righteous Practices: The Moral Compass

Involving God in the business process also encourages ethical practices. By consciously dedicating a portion of profits to divine causes, business owners align their actions with a higher moral purpose. This belief naturally guides them towards honesty, integrity, and fairness in their dealings, ensuring that business is conducted in a way that reflects high moral standards. The ethical implications of this practice ensure that business growth is accompanied by growth in character.

A Legacy of Responsibility and Integrity

In the Marwari community, business is not just about making money – it is about creating a legacy of responsibility and ethical conduct. By embedding God into the fabric of business, there is a constant drive to channel business success towards creating a positive impact on the world. This legacy goes beyond wealth; it reflects a business built on values that serve the greater good.

A Window into My Experiences

I believe making God a partner in business instils a deep sense of confidence, purpose, and belonging. It connects entrepreneurs to their roots and integrates philanthropy as a natural extension of their business practices.

From my personal experience, this philosophy goes beyond the modern concept of Corporate Social Responsibility (CSR) and transforms into 'Community's Shared Responsibility'.

Philanthropy, in this sense, is not just an obligation but a way of life. It becomes part of the business's goodwill. Even small acts of giving contribute to this goodwill, and the more goodwill you create, the more opportunities come your way. People trust you more, partnerships flourish, and your business grows naturally.

Now it's Your Turn!

Adopting this *lokokti* can be transformative, not only in terms of business growth, but in creating a meaningful legacy rooted in integrity, trust, and community engagement. Here are some actionable steps:

1. **Dedicate a percentage of profits to charitable causes:** Commit 1-2% of your annual profit to charity or social causes. This can be directed to religious institutions, community development projects, or causes that align with your values.

2. **Implement automatic ways of giving back:** Introduce an autopilot system for giving, where a percentage of every sale or transaction automatically goes towards a cause you care about. Offer customers an option to participate in this giving back system, such as rounding up their bill or choosing a cause they want to support through their purchase.

***

Chapter 50

Bund bund se gharo bhare

(बूँद बूँद से घड़ो भरे)

————— ❖ —————

A proverb on the power of small steps and incremental growth

Drop by Drop, the Pot Fills

This Marwari proverb beautifully captures the above idea.

But it also has a deeper meaning: success is never defined by grand gestures or overnight achievements but by the steady accumulation of small efforts. It is a principle that resonates deeply with entrepreneurs, individuals striving for personal growth, and anyone working towards long-term goals.

Every Small Contribution Matters

In business, small earnings and consistent efforts can create immense value over time. Whether you are building a company from scratch or pursuing a personal goal, even the smallest steps can add up to something significant.

Think of each drop as a small win – a satisfied customer, a saved rupee, or a process improvement. While each may seem insignificant in isolation, together they form the foundation of sustainable success.

The Hidden Strength of Compounding

This proverb perfectly captures the essence of compounding: the way small actions or investments grow exponentially over time. For example, in business, consistent improvements in service or product quality can gradually build a reputation that sets you apart. Similarly, small savings reinvested wisely can lead to substantial financial growth.

Compounding also applies to personal habits. Ten minutes of daily reading can lead to a wealth of knowledge over the years, just as practising a skill regularly can transform your expertise.

Small Steps, Big Vision

The true wisdom of *bund bund se gharo bhare* lies in the balance between focusing on daily actions and staying aligned with a larger purpose. This is closely linked to the Japanese philosophy of Kaizen, which emphasises continuous improvement through small, actionable changes.

- **In business:** Break down your big goals into manageable tasks. Want to expand your market? Start by reaching out to one potential customer a day. Want to improve efficiency? Begin by tweaking one workflow. Over time, these small adjustments can transform your business.

- **In personal life:** Commit to incremental habits, such as waking up ten minutes earlier or dedicating a small amount of time daily to a skill. These efforts, however small, can compound into noticeable results.

A Window into My Experiences

'Thinking big while acting small' is the most effective way to manage risk – something I have learnt firsthand, and it remains just as relevant today. In business, outcomes are often unpredictable, so the wisest approach is to pair a bold vision with incremental, thoughtful steps. This helps you aim high while maintaining control over the process. The guiding philosophy should always be: Tomorrow should be better than yesterday.

If you leap all in at once, your ability to take risks diminishes significantly because you have more at stake at any given moment. By advancing step by step, you reduce exposure to potential setbacks and simultaneously create room for adjustments, learning, and sustainable growth along the way.

Now it's Your Turn!

Embracing this philosophy can build a solid foundation for long-term success. Here are some actionable steps:

1. **Set micro-goals:** Break down long-term objectives into smaller, achievable targets. Monitor progress consistently.

2. **Save and reinvest:** Allocate a portion of your profits for future growth rather than short-term gratification.

3. **Avoid over-leverage:** Take on manageable risks, ensure your debt-to-income ratio remains healthy and prioritise investments with clear, sustainable returns.

4. **Small gestures matter:** Regular follow-ups, personalised communication, and occasional small tokens of appreciation can build lasting customer loyalty.

5. **Choose consistency over perfection:** Deliver reliable service, even in small steps, rather than aiming for immediate perfection.

***

Chapter 51

Dariya ko paani dariya mein

(दरिया को पानी दरिया में)

※

A proverb that draws inspiration from nature to shape corporate governance

The Water of the River Eventually Flows Back into the River

The proverb *dariya ko paani dariya mein* reflects the idea of cycles, balance, and return, offering profound lessons for corporate governance. Just as nature governs itself through intricate and harmonious cycles, so too should businesses aspire to manage their resources and relationships in ways that are ethical, sustainable, and beneficial to all stakeholders.

Governance in Nature

In nature, the water cycle is a timeless example of governance at its finest. The sun evaporates water from rivers and seas,

240

transforming it into clouds. These clouds release rain, nourishing life across the land – plants grow, animals thrive, and ecosystems flourish. Yet, this rain does not just vanish; it eventually flows back into rivers and seas, completing the cycle. This natural rhythm is efficient as well as deeply equitable, as it benefits a wide array of life before returning to its source. Corporate governance can (and should) mirror this process.

Creating Value in Business

In business, shareholders provide capital, much like the oceans provide water. This capital is the lifeblood that allows enterprises to grow, innovate, and expand. But growth is not the end of the story.

Just as the water that rains upon the earth enriches and sustains life, the value generated by a business must create prosperity beyond its immediate boundaries. This means creating jobs, advancing innovation, fostering societal well-being and driving economic growth. Eventually, however, the wealth and value created must find their way back to shareholders, completing the cycle. This is not merely an obligation; it is the essence of trust and sustainability.

The same principle applies to loans and borrowed resources. When businesses take loans, the expectation is not just that the amount will be repaid with interest. There is a deeper responsibility to ensure that this borrowed capital is used productively, creating tangible prosperity along the way. A loan used to build a factory, for example, does not just generate returns for the lender; it also creates jobs, stimulates local economies, and contributes to societal development. The repayment of the loan, in this sense, is only one part of a much larger, more meaningful cycle.

Sustaining the Cycle

Corporate governance, like the water cycle, should emphasise continuity. It is not a one-time transaction but an ongoing process of taking, transforming, and giving back. Just as rain falls year after year, enriching life in each season, businesses must continuously reinvest in their operations, their people, and their communities. This ensures that the cycle remains unbroken and that the benefits flow not just to a select few but to all who depend on the organisation in one way or another.

A Window into My Experiences

Over the past thirty years of my professional journey, I have been investing in shares, and one observation stands out clearly: companies that prioritise returning value to their shareholders – whether through consistent dividends or significant business growth – are the ones that truly flourish. This approach mirrors the natural governance system of rain and water, where resources circulate, benefit all, and replenish themselves. It profoundly reflects how nature achieves balance and sustains value over time.

This philosophy also captures the essence of corporate responsibility. Businesses, like rivers, draw from various sources – shareholders, bankers, employees, and society at large. In return, it becomes the business's duty to give back, and not just equally but abundantly. Whatever is taken must be amplified and returned, enriching all those involved.

This principle is deeply rooted in *Sanatan* philosophy, an enduring truth that has guided civilisations for centuries and will continue to do so.

Nature teaches us that true prosperity is not diminished by sharing. Just as a river nourishes everything in its path and still retains its vitality, a well-governed business creates value at every stage while maintaining its own strength and purpose.

Now it's Your Turn!

Create a governance model rooted in balance, sustainability, and shared prosperity. Every drop of effort counts; here are some actionable steps:

1. **Capitalise wisely:** Use shareholder investments or loans for productive activities that directly contribute to business growth.

2. **Plan for returns:** Design business models that provide tangible returns to stakeholders, such as profits for shareholders or repaid loans with clear outcomes for lenders.

3. **Create local impact:** Support the local community through job creation and collaborations with small vendors.

***

Chapter 52

Desh ki aan, Bhamashah ki shaan
(देश की आन, भामाशाह की शान)

A saying on the legacy of contribution and pride

The Country's Pride is *Bhamashah's* Glory

This saying celebrates the enduring legacy of a Marwari merchant named *Bhamashah* whose contributions left an indelible mark on both his community and the nation. The proverb honours *Bhamashah's* historical acts of selflessness.

It also teaches how individual contributions can shape the larger fabric of society, offering a valuable lesson for businesses today.

The rise of *Bhamashah*

Bhamashah, a figure of immense stature in the 16th-century Mewar region of Rajasthan, is remembered for his exceptional leadership, generosity, and civic responsibility. Hailing from a respected family of traders, *Bhamashah* amassed substantial wealth. However, what truly defined his legacy was not his fortune but the profound impact he had through his actions. He used his wealth to serve the greater good, prioritising the welfare of his people and his country over personal gain.

His most pivotal moment came when he became a key ally of Maharana Pratap, the revered Rajput king fighting to preserve the sovereignty of Mewar against the Mughal Empire. Amidst a severe financial crisis during the war, when many others abandoned the Maharana, *Bhamashah* made an extraordinary gesture. He donated his entire fortune – gold, jewels, and precious resources – to fund the military campaign. This selfless act provided critical resources to sustain the Rajput resistance and reaffirmed his unwavering commitment to the Rajput cause.

The Enduring Legacy

Bhamashah's generosity and leadership earned him a lasting place in history. His story is passed down through generations as a model of how personal wealth and influence can be used to benefit society. To this day, his name is synonymous with selflessness and philanthropy.

Bhamashah's legacy transcends time, inspiring individuals and businesses alike to understand that true success is measured by the positive impact one leaves on the world.

Selfless Contributions and Civic Responsibility

Bhamashah's life teaches us that wealth and resources are not solely for personal gain. In today's business world, this principle is especially relevant. Companies should focus not only on profitability but also on their broader impact on employees, customers, and the community. A business that contributes to the well-being of society builds a foundation of trust and respect, which in turn nurtures long-term success.

By investing in their communities and driving national progress, businesses play a crucial role in shaping the future of their countries. Just as *Bhamashah's* wealth supported the Rajput cause, businesses today can contribute to national growth through their operations, products, and services.

The Role of Leadership in Inspiring a Legacy

Bhamashah's contributions were driven by his visionary leadership. He understood that true leadership is about setting a direction for the greater good and inspiring others to follow. In business, the values and vision of a leader shape the entire organisation.

A strong leader can instil a culture of integrity, service, and responsibility, which ultimately drives the business's long-term success. Just as *Bhamashah's* leadership inspired his community, business leaders today have the power to create a lasting legacy by prioritising values over profits and contributing meaningfully to society.

The Power of Collective

Bhamashah's influence was not just a result of his wealth but also the goodwill and respect he earned from the people he helped and the community he served. His generosity created a ripple effect, uniting people around a common cause.

Similarly, in the business world, success is rarely the product of leadership alone; it is a collective effort. Employees, suppliers, customers, and investors all play pivotal roles in shaping and sustaining a business's achievements.

The more a business fosters collaboration, mutual respect, and shared goals, the stronger and more sustainable its impact will be. Like *Bhamashah*, whose generosity is supported by the community, businesses thrive when they engage all stakeholders in their mission and contribute to a collective vision for the greater good.

A Window into My Experiences

In Marwari culture, anyone who donates their wealth or time for the betterment of society or the nation is often referred to as a *Bhamashah*, in honour of Maharana Pratap's legendary ally who exemplified selflessness and service. This recognition celebrates the act of giving back and highlights its profound impact on personal and professional growth.

When you give back to society, you naturally enhance your personal brand and boost your business's value. Acts of generosity and responsibility create goodwill, attract talented individuals, strengthen market presence, and even elevate your reputation (*izzat*) in the business world. This goodwill becomes a powerful intangible asset, building trust and reliability among stakeholders.

This philosophy is inherently cyclical. As businesses earn wealth from society, they reinvest it into their communities, building stronger relationships and earning reputational capital in return. This enhanced reputation empowers businesses with greater efficiency, broader opportunities, and sustained success. Much like nature's cycles, the act of giving creates a self-reinforcing loop where everyone benefits – businesses, individuals, and society as a whole.

Now it's Your Turn!

You too can follow *Bhamashah's* footsteps. Here are some actions you can take:

1. **Commit to corporate social responsibility (CSR):** Start by identifying key areas in which you can contribute to the community. This could include supporting local education, sponsoring health initiatives, or investing in sustainability.

2. **Engage employees in social causes:** Create a culture where employees feel encouraged to participate in charitable activities, with the business backing those efforts.

3. **Foster national pride through brand purpose:** Align the company's mission with national values. Whether it's hiring local talent, supporting Indian-made products or contributing to green initiatives, you should take pride in being a force that enhances national pride, just as *Bhamashah* did.

***

Chapter 53

Aaj ki thaperi aaj koni bale

(आज की थपेरी आज कोनी बले)

A proverb on patience and the importance of process

Can You Use Today's Cow Dung as Fuel?

This Marwari proverb carries profound lessons about patience, process, and timing.

In India, cow dung is collected, shaped into patties, and dried in the sun before it is burned as fuel. The drying process typically takes 3-4 days, and until it is complete, the patties cannot be used effectively in a fire.

The proverb tells us that certain processes cannot be rushed, and attempting to shortcut them can lead to inefficiency and failure.

Aaj ki thaperi (today's cow dung) *aaj koni bale* (cannot fuel today's fire).

The simple wisdom transcends its rural origins and resonates deeply in the world of business and life. Here's how.

A Lesson in Patience

At its core, the *lokokti* emphasises the importance of patience and understanding the natural flow of progress. Just as cow dung must dry thoroughly before it can serve as an effective fuel, any endeavour – be it in business, relationships, or personal growth – requires time to mature.

In a world that often demands instant results, this adage reminds us to respect the process and trust that outcomes will come when the time is right.

The Business Angle: Rushing Leads to Waste

In the business context, the proverb has powerful applications:

1. **Product development**:

   A rushed product launch can lead to errors, dissatisfied customers, and potential reputational damage. Like drying cow dung, every phase of development – research, testing, refinement – must be given its due time.

2. **Team building**:

   Building a strong, cohesive team is not an overnight task. It involves nurturing talent, building trust, and creating a culture where collaboration thrives. Skipping steps or pushing too hard too soon can lead to burnout and discontent.

3. **Strategic decisions**:

Quick decisions driven by urgency rather than strategy often backfire. Successful businesses take the time to analyse, plan, and execute carefully.

Above All, Trust the Process

The wisdom of the *lokokti* aligns with nature's rhythms. Crops take time to grow, rivers take years to carve valleys, and even the mightiest tree starts as a seed. Nature does not rush, yet everything is accomplished in its time.

Businesses that respect this natural order – investing in gradual growth and understanding the value of patience – build a foundation for lasting success.

A Window into My Experiences

Business is inherently imaginative. You need to dream big and then execute your vision, step by step. Learning from the past and building for the future is important. Remember, what you sow today, you reap tomorrow.

I often reflect on a unique version of the word 'industry': in-dust-tree. Every business is essentially planting a tree in the dust. It takes time. First, you plant the seed, then you wait, and finally, you reap the rewards. I have witnessed this firsthand. Persistence and patience are undoubtedly the hallmarks of great business leaders. My own journey has reinforced this truth: businesses are built brick by brick.

Now it's Your Turn!

The proverb is rich with wisdom, offering a deep metaphor rooted in the rhythms of traditional life. Here are some actionable steps inspired by it:

1. **Plan before you act**: Conduct feasibility studies or pilot projects to test your ideas before full-scale implementation.

2. **Develop gradually, not overnight:** Focus on building a solid customer base and gradually scaling your operations. For example, prioritise perfecting one product or market before diversifying.

3. **Learn to pause and reflect:** Incorporate regular review meetings into your operations to assess progress and adjust strategies as needed.

***

Chapter 54

Sapna se pet koni bhare

(सपना से पेट कोनी भरे)

—◆◆—

A saying on balancing vision with practicality

Dreams Cannot Fill Your Stomach

This *lokokti* is about balancing aspiration and action. While having a grand vision is essential for progress and growth, it is equally important to address immediate needs and ensure the basics are taken care of.

This saying encourages leaders, especially in business, to strike a balance between ambitious goals and the practical, day-to-day necessities of running an enterprise.

Big Dreams and Real Challenges

A business thrives on its vision – the long-term aspirations that guide decision-making, innovation, and growth. However, focusing solely on the future can lead to neglecting the present. Employees, customers, and stakeholders rely on a business not just for its potential but for what it delivers today.

For example:

- **Employees need timely salaries and resources** to perform their duties, no matter how promising the company's future might look.

- **Customers expect quality products or services now,** not just promises of innovation down the road.

- **Investors and stakeholders need evidence of steady progress** alongside long-term potential.

Ignoring these immediate needs in favour of lofty dreams can lead to dissatisfaction, instability, and even failure.

The Dual Lens of Leadership

Great leaders recognise the importance of keeping one eye on the horizon and the other on the ground. They dream big but act small, ensuring that while they work towards their long-term vision, they are also addressing the immediate needs of their team and business.

This balance is especially important for small and medium enterprises, where resources are often limited and risks are high. An entrepreneur with a dream of global expansion must also ensure their current operations are sustainable, profitable, and meeting stakeholder expectations.

A Window into My Experiences

My experience building businesses has taught me a valuable lesson: while grand visions, inspiring speeches, and flashy projections may capture attention, the foundation of any successful enterprise lies in meeting immediate needs. Everyone requires basic necessities like food and shelter, and the pursuit of long-term goals must be balanced with short-term rewards and recognition.

I have always aimed to create businesses that foster both individual and collective growth. My goal is to see myself and my employees experience significant financial rewards in the long run. However, I also recognise the importance of immediate gratification. We all need to live comfortably, travel with family, and enjoy the fruits of our labour along the way.

While some team members may be driven purely by the long-term goal, it is important to ensure everyone feels valued and rewarded for their contributions.

Now it's Your Turn!

Sapna se pet koni bhare is not a rejection of ambition; it is a call to action. In the end, it is not just dreams that define your journey, but how well you manage the realities of today while working towards the possibilities of tomorrow.

Consider these steps:

- **For employee retention:** Regular feedback, achievable milestones and a sense of purpose tied to everyday tasks can keep employees motivated and engaged.

- **For customer loyalty:** Delivering consistent value and reliability can keep customers returning while you work on transformative changes.

- **For financial stability:** Addressing short-term cash flow and operational challenges can create the foundation for long-term growth.

***

Chapter 55

Andha mein kano sardar

(अंधा में काणो सरदार)

An adage on relative value in business

In the Crowd of the Blind, the One-Eyed Man is King

Value, power, and prominence are almost always contextual. The world of business is no exception.

The understanding of demand, supply, and customer segments to position oneself effectively maximises opportunities.

Eyes on Relative Value

The proverb recognises that what stands out as 'valuable' depends on the surrounding context. In a marketplace filled with options of similar or lower quality, even a slightly superior offering can gain prominence and command a premium. This relativity plays a key role in business strategy, especially when it comes to pricing, positioning, and market segmentation.

For example, a cup of tea is sold at drastically different prices depending on where it is served – a five-star hotel, an airport, a cinema hall, or a roadside stall. The product may be the same, but the value is perceived differently based on the environment, convenience, and the customer's expectations.

A business offering modest innovation in a niche market can still dominate if the alternatives are less appealing or non-existent.

The Theory of Demand, Supply, and Perception

In business, demand, and supply are not just economic concepts; they are deeply influenced by perception and context.

- **Customer segments matter:** What works for one segment may not appeal to another. A premium service might thrive in an urban setting but fail in a rural market with different priorities and spending capacities.

- **Pricing strategies:** Understanding how customers perceive value helps businesses price their products or services appropriately. For example, a luxury brand can charge a premium by emphasising exclusivity, while a mass-market product relies on affordability.

- **Innovation v/s necessity:** Even small innovations can hold immense value in a context where alternatives are outdated or inefficient. For example, introducing low-cost solar lanterns in rural areas where kerosene lamps are the primary light source can transform lives by providing a safer, cleaner, and more cost-effective solution.

A Window into My Experiences

We often get caught up in the idea that we need to be unique and have a flawless product. While differentiation can be beneficial, it is equally important to focus on meeting market demand.

If there is a strong demand for a product, even if your offering is not perfect, you can still succeed as long as it is competitive. The key is to ensure your supply matches the demand without overproducing.

I learnt this firsthand during my second venture. Many people questioned our ability to compete with large corporations. However, I realised that in our specific market, being the biggest player was not necessarily the key to survival. Instead, it was about having patience, a clear purpose, and a keen understanding of the market's needs.

Now it's Your Turn!

In a world driven by perception, remember being 'the best' is often less important than being 'better enough' to stand out. Here are some actionable steps:

1. **Understand your market segments:** Conduct surveys, interviews, or focus groups to understand customer preferences and pain points. Avoid trying to please everyone. Focus on a niche where your relative advantage is the strongest.

2. **Embrace strategic pricing:** Use tiered pricing models to appeal to different customer segments (e.g., budget-friendly,

mid-range, and premium). Analyse competitors' pricing and position yourself competitively within your chosen segment. You can also experiment with value-based pricing. For example, if you offer unique convenience or time savings, charge a premium.

***

Chapter 56

Aapko gaon aur cheez ka dam aayisi

(आपको गाँव और चीज़ का दाम आएसी)

A proverb on true value and the cycles of stability

The Journey Back to True Value

This Marwari proverb provides insights into the nature of value, stability, and the wisdom of long-term thinking. Just as a person, no matter how far they travel, always returns to their village, commodities, investments, or opportunities eventually return to their intrinsic value after periods of excitement or momentum.

It is important to understand the underlying 'fundamental value', avoid the pitfalls of temporary hype, and be patient in both life and business.

Stability is Inevitable

This *lokokti* highlights two key ideas:

- Avoid getting swept up in temporary excitement or irrational exuberance

- Focus on long-term fundamentals instead of short-term gains

Whether in financial investments, business decisions, or personal endeavours, the lesson is to respect the underlying factors that drive true worth.

A Broader Perspective: Of Nature and Cycles

The proverb also aligns with the cycles of nature. Rivers flow to the ocean but are ultimately drawn back to their source through evaporation and rainfall. Similarly, markets, relationships, and life decisions go through ups and downs but return to a state of equilibrium.

In business, this means respecting cycles of growth and contraction. It is not just about riding the highs but also preparing for the lows.

A Window into My Experiences

From my experience, the adage 'time in the market, not timing the market' has been key for investing in stocks, gold, or even real estate. Humans have a natural tendency to follow trends. When gold prices are consistently rising, many people tend to invest at the peak, believing it is the optimal time. However, this often leads to investing at inflated prices.

Similarly, in the stock market, retail investors frequently buy at market highs, paying premium prices, rather than investing systematically over time. This approach can result in significant losses or minimal returns.

It is wiser to invest in valuations aligned with fundamental value, rather than chase momentum. Whenever I have succumbed to the temptation of momentum investing, I have inevitably faced losses.

To counter this impulse, I have used a strategy: if a stock's price is inflated due to momentum, I would create a fixed deposit for the equivalent amount. This way, I would maintain my investment discipline without actually buying the overpriced stock. Eventually, when the stock price corrected to its fundamental value, I would withdraw from the fixed deposit and invest in the stock. This approach offered two advantages: I earned interest on the fixed deposit during the interim, and I effectively reduced my investment cost by buying at a lower price.

Valuable assets always revert to their intrinsic value over time.

Now it's Your Turn!

In a world that often celebrates speed, this proverb encourages us to take the long view, respect cycles, and ultimately, return to what truly sustains us. Here are some actionable steps:

1. **Understand the true value:** Conduct thorough market research to determine whether the demand for a product or service is genuine and sustainable. Avoid making decisions based on temporary popularity or market speculation.

2. **Avoid overpaying for momentum:** Develop a strategy for assessing the true worth of acquisitions or investments. For example, look at the historical pricing, intrinsic utility, and long-term prospects of a commodity before committing resources.

3. **Invest with a margin of safety:** If a resource's price is soaring due to demand, wait for the hype to settle before making a purchase.

4. **Learn to pause and reflect:** If competitors are rushing into a new trend, take the time to evaluate its longevity before jumping in.

***

Chapter 57

Gallo ginkar ghara chaal

(गल्लौ गिणकर घरा चाल)

------***------

*A proverb on financial discipline and
work-life balance*

Count Your Cash, Then Go Home

The *lokokti* of this chapter translates to exactly this.

It carries valuable lessons about responsibility, balance, and the importance of peace in life. It speaks to two key aspects: financial discipline and the need for a work-life balance.

Accountability and Peace

The first part of the proverb, 'count your cash' (*gallo ginkar*) highlights the importance of financial accountability. Before you finish your work for the day and head home, make sure you have a clear understanding of your finances. Whether it is in business or personal life, keeping track of resources, money, and commitments ensures that everything is in order. This financial mindfulness prevents any surprises and helps avoid potential conflicts later.

The second part, 'return home' (*ghara chaal*), spotlights the significance of peace and rest after work. After the hustle of the day, it is important to disconnect from work and find calm in the comfort of home. It suggests that work and personal life should be kept in balance, with work concluding in a way that brings you peace and harmony when you return home.

The Broader Lesson: Peace Comes After Accountability

At its core, this proverb also teaches us that financial and personal responsibility go hand in hand with peace of mind. A well-balanced life, both in terms of finances and personal well-being, allows for greater focus and productivity at work and a sense of calm when at home.

A Window into My Experiences

I have always adhered to this principle in both my professional and personal life. I maintain a strict record of my finances, tracking both income and expenses. Whether it is through traditional methods or modern tools like Enterprise Resource Planning (ERP) and Artificial Intelligence (AI), daily monitoring is important.

As we have discussed in one of our earlier chapters '*Taka toh tem ko tabar hai*' – time is money, and the power of compounding is undeniable. Diligently follow accounting principles and risk management strategies to harness the full potential of your investments.

Now it's Your Turn!

Before you end your day, you must take stock of your financial situation, ensuring that your business is on track and that all accounts are in order. Here are some actionable steps:

1. Establish financial discipline:

- **Daily/weekly financial check-ins**: As a business owner, it is important to keep a close eye on your cash flow. Set aside specific times during the day or week to review your financials: check accounts receivable, review expenses, and ensure you are on top of your cash flow.

- **Ensure cash flow stability**: Cash flow is the lifeblood of any business. Ensure that your cash flow remains positive by timely invoicing, following up on overdue payments, and keeping operating costs under control.

2. Separate work from personal life:

- **Set boundaries for work hours**: Create clear boundaries between work and personal time. Set specific work hours and stick to them. This prevents burnout and ensures you have time to unwind.

- **Delegate to empower**: As your business grows, trust your team members with responsibilities. Do not carry the weight of the business on your shoulders alone. Empower your employees to take on tasks, which will allow you to step away from work when needed without compromising business performance.

***

Chapter 58

Vyaapar ka teen dhani – izzat, rokra aur guni

(व्यापार का तीन धनी – इज़्ज़त, रोकड़ा और गुणी)

———— ❖ ————

A proverb on the three key building blocks for a successful business

One Business, Three Pillars

Businesses, now and throughout history, have stood on three fundamental pillars: reputation, cash flow, and skill. Each of these elements plays a vital role in creating a successful and sustainable enterprise.

Let's see how.

The Power of *Izzat*

Reputation (*izzat*) is foundational in the business world. It shapes how customers, partners, and competitors view you. Building a reputation for honesty and reliability builds trust and loyalty. When customers feel valued, they are more likely to return and recommend your business to others. Plus, fostering mutual respect among your team creates a vibrant work culture that encourages collaboration and boosts morale.

Rokra is Your Business Lifeblood

Cash flow (*rokra*) is crucial for any business to thrive. Money is what keeps the lights on and fuels your growth. Balance your income and expenses wisely to maintain financial health. Smart budgeting and strategic investments help you weather tough times and position you for new opportunities. After all, having the right funding can open doors to exciting projects and expansions.

Gunn is Your Competitive Advantage

Skill (*gunn*) and skilled people (*guni*) drive your business forward. This encompasses both industry-specific knowledge and essential soft skills like leadership and communication. Investing in training and continuous learning increases your team's capabilities and sparks innovation. A skilled workforce can quickly adapt to changes in the market and better meet customer needs, keeping your business ahead of the competition.

A Window into My Experiences

Just as the heart, blood and kidneys work in harmony to sustain the human body, these three pillars must coexist for a business to flourish. Throughout my experiences with Microsec and

SastaSundar, *izzat* has always been the heart of doing business. However, upholding our reputation was only possible when we had sufficient cash flow to support operations.

Thus, generating *rokra* was also a vital aspect of business sustainability, but it took its own time and strategic planning to manifest. I realised that without adequate cash flow, a business struggles to survive, just as the body cannot function without a proper supply of blood.

Equally important has been the role of *guni*. Just as kidneys filter waste and maintain balance within the body, intelligent manpower and advanced technology have ensured that our businesses cut through the noise and stand out in the market.

Hence, no single element – *izzat, rokra* or *guni* – is more important than the others. They are interdependent and equally essential for success.

Now it's Your Turn!

Apply the saying's wisdom in your enterprise. Here are some actionable steps:

Build Reputation

- **Cultivate a transparent culture:** Transparency in decision-making and communication builds trust within your team and with customers. Share both successes and challenges openly to build a culture of respect.

- **Understand your customers deeply:** Take the time to learn about your customers' needs and preferences. Tailored interactions strengthen loyalty and turn your customers into passionate supporters of your brand.

Manage Cash Flow

- **Broaden your revenue sources:** Seek out alternative income streams, such as introducing new offerings or subscription services that cater to evolving customer preferences. This provides a buffer against market volatility.

- **Regularly assess your financial health:** Make it a habit to review your finances monthly. By closely monitoring cash flow, margins, and expenditures, you can identify emerging trends and act before potential issues arise.

Enhance Skills

- **Hire intelligent people:** Prioritise recruiting individuals with diverse skill sets and critical thinking abilities. Intelligent hires bring fresh perspectives and innovative solutions to the table. Look for candidates who demonstrate a willingness to learn and adapt.

- **Create a learning roadmap:** Develop personalised learning plans for employees based on their roles and career aspirations. This targeted approach ensures that skill development aligns with both individual goals and organisational needs.

***

Chapter 59

Izzat ka teen dhani – niyam, kayda aur gurh ki vani

(इज़्ज़त का तीन धनी – नियम, कायदा और गुड़ की वाणी)

———— ❖ ————

A proverb highlighting the three key elements of maintaining a business's reputation

The Blueprint to a Lasting Reputation

This *lokokti* flows directly from our earlier proverb on *izzat* (reputation), one of the pillars of a successful business.

As you know, a reputation is not built overnight, nor can it be maintained without committing to strong core values. *Izzat* also has three pillars of its own, which are essential in guiding you on this journey. Let's understand them.

Niyam (Regulations)

The first pillar is *niyam*, or compliance with regulations. The laws of the land are not just guidelines – they are the foundation of your business's legitimacy. If you violate these laws, whether they come from the government, corporate policies or internal frameworks, your reputation can come crashing down in an instant. A single misstep can lead to legal penalties, but more critically, it can destroy the trust that your business has worked hard to earn. This trust is indispensable. It is what assures stakeholders that your operations are reliable and honourable, making it the backbone of long-term success.

Kayda (Ethics)

While regulations set the external framework, *kayda* – ethical business conduct – goes deeper. It lies beyond adhering to imposed rules but setting high standards for yourself. Ethics determine how you interact with every stakeholder, from your customers to shareholders to employees. Treating people with respect, prioritising transparency and ensuring that profit does not come at the expense of principles are what define a truly ethical business. This is how you earn trust and differentiate yourself in a competitive market.

Gurh ki Vani (Graceful Communication)

Then there is *gurh ki vani*, the art of communication, which is as vital as the previous two pillars. No matter how compliant or ethical your business is, if your communication is harsh or careless, it can undermine all your efforts. A business's voice should be respectful and considerate, much like the sweetness of jaggery. Every interaction – whether with employees, customers, or partners – should reflect kindness and clarity.

At the end of the day, it is effective communication that builds bridges, fosters understanding, and creates lasting relationships.

A Window into My Experiences

Back in the Microsec days, reputation was critical for us. People entrusted their money to our asset management company because they believed in us. The same was true with SastaSundar, where we dealt with life-saving medicines and healthcare products – trust was not just important; it was essential.

Today, businesses are more closely scrutinised than ever. It is more than just about adhering to written laws. It is about aligning with the unwritten rules society expects us to follow. This makes all three elements – compliance, ethical integrity, and graceful communication – non-negotiable for sustaining any venture.

Mistakes will happen, sometimes unknowingly. You might face a legal slip-up or find yourself compromising on ethics. Instead of getting defensive, the smartest move is to own up to it, communicate openly, and take responsibility. This approach will prevent further damage and reinforce your reputation and credibility. In the end, it is how you handle these moments that define your success.

Now it's Your Turn!

This proverb can serve as a guiding framework for your business decisions and growth. Let me break it down into actionable steps that you can implement:

1. Build a Compliance Culture for *Niyam*

- **Understand industry regulations:** Whether it is financial, healthcare or any other sector, you must be aware of the specific regulations that apply to your industry. Ensure you have a dedicated team or individual to monitor compliance.

- **Conduct regular audits:** Implement routine audits to check for any regulatory risks. Startups, especially, can sometimes be more vulnerable to penalties due to a lack of resources. Proactively addressing this ensures you are prepared for any scrutiny.

Think of regulations as the foundation of a house. Without them, the entire structure can collapse. Compliance protects both your reputation and your long-term sustainability.

2. Build with Integrity for *Kayda*

- **Establish ethical guidelines:** Every business, no matter how small, should have a code of ethics. These guidelines should cover areas like transparency with clients, honesty in pricing and fair treatment of employees.

- **Lead by example:** As the leader, your actions set the tone for your business. Model the ethical behaviour you want to see in your employees. Ensure that your business decisions benefit not only the bottom line but also your stakeholders. Your personal integrity will trickle down into the entire organisation.

But ethical conduct is not just about ticking boxes; it is about staying true to your internal moral compass and ensuring you never fall short of your own standards.

3. Build Positive Relationships for *Gurh ki Vani*

- **Communicate with care:** Whether you are dealing with employees, clients or partners, always communicate with respect and clarity. A kind tone builds relationships that can last a lifetime.

- **Resolve conflicts gracefully:** Challenges are inevitable, but how you handle them will define your reputation. Address conflicts with patience and strategy to maintain your standing in the market.

Communication is the glue that holds everything together. In today's fast-paced business reality, a respectful, well-spoken leader will always stand out and foster strong relationships.

***

Chapter 60

Rokra ka teen dhani – munafo, bachat aur chalto paani

(रोकड़ा का तीन धनी – मुनाफ़ो, बचत और चालतो पानी)

— ❦ —

A wise saying on the three key elements of sustaining a business's cash flow

The Three Pillars of Financial Health

As we explored in a previous chapter, cash flow (*rokra*) is the lifeblood of any business, and managing it well is what keeps an enterprise alive and thriving. The proverb of this chapter presents a clear framework for managing *rokra* effectively.

It focuses on these three essential ingredients:

Munafo (Profit)

First and foremost, we have profit – the bedrock of any successful business. But it is not just about generating any profit – it is about consistently creating sustainable profit. Sustainable profit means you have built something solid enough to withstand market fluctuations, competition, and unforeseen challenges.

In today's world of unicorn startups, many businesses chase growth at the cost of profitability, but the truth is that without profit, your business is like a car running out of fuel. Profit does not just keep your business running; it helps you to invest back into your operations, expand and improve. A business that focuses on building a long-term profitable model ensures a steady and reliable cash flow.

Bachat (Savings)

But profit alone is not enough; it is what you do with that profit that matters. In the same way that individuals need personal savings, businesses need to manage their cash reserves carefully.

A positive cash flow does not mean you should spend everything – it means you have the foresight to save for future investments and unexpected downturns. Savings act as a buffer, enabling your business to weather storms without stalling. When the market contracts or opportunities for growth arise, your reserves will help you act swiftly and strategically. This also ensures you have capital on hand to invest in expansion when the time is right.

Chalto Paani (Flowing Operations)

Finally, we have the idea of *chalto paani*. Just like water that stagnates becomes unhealthy, a business that loses its operational flow starts to decay. Continuity in operations is critical – even when things are not going perfectly, your business must keep moving.

Success rarely comes from massive leaps; it often comes from constant, small steps forward. This flow can take the form of maintaining regular sales, keeping customer relationships strong, or consistently innovating and improving processes.

In fact, we have explored this insight in one of our previous chapters as well – *chako ghumto pako* – the wheel of business, like the wheel of life, must keep turning.

A Window into My Experiences

I personally prioritise cash flow, as it is a fundamental ingredient for business success. When cash flow is limited, you may find yourself compromising on the larger interests of your business. So, it is essential to keep a close eye on your cash composition, preserve your cash reserves and invest wisely.

In personal life too, capital allocation is critical – you want to ensure that your money is working hard for you and generating the best possible returns. These returns should then be reinvested in other profit-generating businesses or opportunities. When done effectively, capital allocation can have a significant impact on your growth and long-term sustainability.

Now it's Your Turn!

Focus on the long game. Short-term wins are important, but sustainable growth, financial security, and operational consistency are what will set you apart in the market. Here are some actionable steps to help you:

1. Focus on Sustainable Profits for *Munafo*

- **Balance revenue growth and margin:** Revenue growth and stable margins are equally important for a business to succeed. Both are interconnected: the more you grow, the more profit you generate.

  However, in the early stages, it might be tempting to chase revenue growth at any cost.

  If you are willing to take risks with your profit margins in pursuit of revenue, make sure you have adequate cash reserves or capital contributions to support that strategy.

  Neglecting to maintain the necessary capital backup can be a risky move, potentially leading to the need to close down the business. Therefore, set your objectives with practicality in mind.

- **Set measurable profit targets:** Establish short-term and long-term profit goals. Break them down into achievable milestones, and review your progress quarterly. This helps you stay focused on building a strong, profitable foundation for your business.

2. Build a Financial Safety Net for *Bachat*

- **Create an emergency fund:** Just as you would in your personal finances, your business needs a rainy-day fund. Set aside a percentage of your profits each month (even if it is small at first) to build a reserve. This fund will help you manage unexpected expenses. Aim to have enough saved to cover at least three to six months of operating expenses.

- **Manage cash flow rigorously:** Always know where your cash is going. Use accounting software to track every inflow and outflow in real time. Avoid making large capital expenditures unless you have planned for them, and ensure your receivables are collected on time. Late payments can suffocate a growing business.

3. Keep Your Business Moving for *Chalto Paani*

- **Focus on consistency:** Consistent, steady operations are the backbone of a successful business. Do not let tough times slow you down. Whether it is maintaining sales, developing new products or simply staying in front of your customers, find ways to keep your business moving – even if it is at a reduced scale. The key is to never let stagnation set in.

***

Chapter 61

Guni ka teen aakhar – santosh, unnati aur aadar

(गुणी का तीन आंखर– संतोष, उन्नति और आदर)

A powerful proverb on the three key elements for building a thriving and respectful workplace

The Building Blocks of Talent

When I talked about the essential ingredients for a successful business, skills and intelligence represented our final pillar. This chapter's proverb delves into the key elements that make up this crucial aspect.

Before we dig in, it is interesting to note the choice of the word *aakhar* here instead of *dhani*, which we have encountered in previous chapters. While *dhani* conveys command, suggesting directives for your business, *aakhar* refers more to the building blocks – much like the alphabet. *Guni ka teen aakhar* then translates to the fundamentals of building a robust talent pool. This distinction adds gravity to this particular proverb, indicating that true talent cannot simply be commanded.

Now, let us explore the key elements that contribute to fostering skills and intelligence within an organisation:

Santosh (Satisfaction)

This lies at the heart of a motivated workforce, and it is non-negotiable for creating a space where employees feel valued and happy in their roles.

To begin with, their compensation must be competitive. Your employees should feel that their salary matches their skills and efforts. If you have performance bonuses tied to market standards, make sure that is communicated clearly. Transparency goes a long way in keeping everyone satisfied.

Moreover, your environment should also be one where employees enjoy doing their work. Establish clear key result areas (KRAs) and key performance indicators (KPIs) so your team knows what is expected. When they see how their work is contributing to the bigger picture, they feel more fulfilled.

A supportive and collaborative workplace culture further enhances job satisfaction. Encourage open conversations and teamwork, creating a space where everyone feels comfortable sharing ideas and feedback.

Unnati (Growth)

The saying "Grow or get left behind" is especially relevant in today's workplace.

To ensure your organisation thrives, consider implementing policies that actively promote personal and professional development for your team. Employee stock ownership plans (ESOPs) can be a game-changer, providing employees with a real stake in the company's success. Such initiatives attract new talent as well as create a sense of ownership and commitment among your existing staff.

Creating opportunities for continuous learning is equally essential. Whether through workshops, online courses, or mentorship, employees appreciate organisations that invest in their development. This commitment to growth uplifts their skills and keeps them engaged.

It is also important to remember that growth is not just about moving up the ladder. Promote programmes that support overall well-being, including health and wellness initiatives. A healthy, balanced workforce is not only more productive but also happier.

Aadar (Respect)

Lastly, let us talk about respect – the most indispensable part of a thriving workplace.

Every employee deserves to be treated with dignity and acknowledgement for their contributions, no matter how small. Building an atmosphere where everyone feels valued is key to building a positive work environment.

And so is creating an inclusive culture that ensures that all voices are heard and respected. Regularly celebrating achievements – big and small – reinforces this sense of appreciation, while encouraging open feedback helps individuals feel recognised for their input. When employees feel respected, it enhances their engagement and loyalty, ultimately driving the success of your organisation.

A Window into My Experiences

I have come across countless posts on workplace portals like LinkedIn, but I have never seen everything encapsulated so perfectly in a single line. This saying truly represents the most important *lokokti* of this book. I can vouch for this wholeheartedly – my own success depends on the incredible team I have with me, and all these elements ring true.

At both our ventures, the company culture has always centred on the concept of 'Being Child'. Just as a child grows each day, we believe in taking small steps forward every day. Like a child learning to play and thrive in a team, we foster a teamwork mindset. Embracing the spirit of fresh young minds, we never discriminate; instead, we make everyone a partner in our business. This partnership approach has been instrumental in building both Microsec and SastaSundar, which are truly people-driven ventures.

Now it's Your Turn!

Investing in your people pays dividends in overall business success. Here are some actionable steps to help you attract top talent and retain your best employees:

1. Enhance Satisfaction for *Santosh*

- **Conduct regular surveys:** Use employee satisfaction surveys to gather insights on what your team values most. This data can help you make informed decisions to improve their experience.

- **Provide flexible work arrangements:** Consider implementing flexible working hours or remote work options. Allowing employees to balance their work and personal lives can significantly boost job satisfaction.

- **Host recognition programmes:** Establish a formal recognition programme that rewards employees for exceptional work. This could include 'Employee of the Month' awards or spot bonuses, which can motivate others to excel.

2. Drive Development for *Unnati*

- **Provide career path planning:** Offer personalised career development plans to your employees. Discuss their aspirations and outline clear paths for advancement within the company.

- **Conduct skill-sharing initiatives:** Organise regular skill-sharing sessions where employees can teach each other new skills or knowledge. This promotes learning as well as strengthens team bonds.

- **Offer networking opportunities:** Facilitate attendance at industry conferences and networking events. Encouraging employees to expand their professional networks can boost their growth and development.

3. Treat with Respect for *Aadar*

- **Set a conflict resolution framework:** Establish clear processes for conflict resolution within the team. Encourage open discussions to address issues respectfully, promoting a harmonious workplace.

- **Encourage inclusive decision-making:** Involve employees in decision-making processes that affect them. This shows respect for their opinions and encourages a sense of ownership and responsibility.

- **Conduct diversity training:** Implement training programmes focused on diversity, equity, and inclusion. Educating your team on the importance of respect for different backgrounds can build a more cohesive work environment.

***

Glossary

Acknowledgement

I extend my heartfelt gratitude to the Marwari entrepreneurs whose wisdom and insights have enriched this book. Their contributions, gathered from everyday conversations, have been invaluable, even as I recognise that perspectives may vary among readers and contributors.

With the utmost respect and admiration, I proudly acknowledge the contributors, whose names are as follows:

Contributor List			
Sl. No.		**Name of Person**	**Company Name**
1	Late	Baijnath Sobhsarla	Rupa Group
2	Late	Mamraj Agarwal	Minu Saree
3	Late	Priyamvada Birla	M.P. Birla Group
4	Late	Sanwar Mal Mittal	Father of the Author
5	Late	Shyam Sunder Beriwala	Shyam Steel Group

Contributor List			
Sl. No.		**Name of Person**	**Company Name**
1	Shri	Aditya Jajodia	Jai Balaji Group
2	Shri	Bhagwati Prasad Jalan	Ganapati Industrial
3	Shri	Bimal Choudhary	Anmol Industries
4	Shri	Bimal Patwari	Pinnacle Infotech
5	Shri	Brij Bhushan Agarwal	Shyam Metalics
6	Shri	Brijesh Beriwala	Shyam Steel Group
7	Shri	Dinesh Adukia	Adukia Group
8	Shri	Ghanshyam Das Agarwal	Adhunik Metaliks
9	Shri	Govardhan Prasad Tantia	GPT Infraprojects
10	Shri	Hari Mohan Bangur	Shree Cement
11	Shri	Indra Chand Bansal	-
12	Shri	Ishwari Prasad Tantia	Tantia Group
13	Shri	Lalit Beriwala	Shyam Steel Group
14	Shri	Mahabir Prasad Jalan	Ramkrishna Forging
15	Shri	Mahavir Prasad Poddar	-
16	Shri	Mahesh Agarwal	Adhunik Industries
17	Shri	Mukesh Bansal	Beekay Steel

18	Shri	Nand Lal Pasari	Primarc Group
19	Shri	Nandlal Rungta	Rungta Mines
20	Shri	Narendra Kumar Daga	Wild Stone
21	Shri	Naveen Vyas	Microsec Wealth
22	Shri	Om Prakash Jalan	Bengal Energy
23	Shri	Prahlad Rai Agarwala	Rupa Group
24	Shri	Radhe Shyam Agarwal	Emami
25	Shri	Radhe Shyam Goenka	Emami
26	Shri	Ram Kishore Bansal	Arya Tea & Eurasia Metaliks
27	Shri	Ranjit Singh Kothari	Kothari Metals
28	Smt.	Ruchika Gupta	Sanmarg
29	Shri	Rajiv Agarwal	Tirupati Vancom
30	Shri	Sajan Kumar Bansal	Skipper
31	Shri	Sajjan Bhajanka	Century Plywood
32	Shri	Sanjay Agarwal	Century Plywood
33	Shri	Sanjiv Goenka	R.P. Sanjiv Goenka Group
34	Shri	Shanti Lal Shrimal	-
35	Shri	Shiv Kumar Lohia	All India Marwari Federation

36	Shri	Shyam Sundar Choudhary	Himadri
37	Shri	Shyam Sunder Agarwal	Srijan Group
38	Shri	Surendra Kumar Dugar	P.S. Group
39	Shri	Surendra Kumar Dugar	BMD Securities
40	Shri	Suresh Agrawal	MSP
41	Shri	Vallabh Bhanshali	Enam Group

I extend my deepest gratitude to my beloved wife, Abha, whose invaluable support has been a constant source of strength and inspiration. Her thoughtful reflections, shared from our morning walks to our dinner table conversations, have enriched this work in countless ways.

My heartfelt thanks also go to my children, Keshav Beriwala, Saloni Mittal Beriwala, Vidhi Mittal, and Krishna Mittal, for their dedicated assistance in the editing process. Their encouragement and meticulous attention to detail have been invaluable.

I am sincerely grateful to Taniya Roy for her remarkable help in translating these words of wisdom, allowing them to resonate with even greater clarity.

Finally, I wish to express my profound appreciation to Ravi Kant Sharma, Rakesh Sony, and Priya Jain Mittal for their invaluable support in refining the manuscript. Their time, care, and expertise have truly enhanced the quality of this work.

Thank you all for being an integral part of this endeavour.

About the Author

Mr. B.L. Mittal, a distinguished entrepreneur and visionary leader, is the founder of healthcare digital platforms, SastaSundar and RetailerShakti, and wealth management firms, Microsec and Club Kautilya. A fellow member of the Institute of Chartered Accountants of India (ICAI), the Institute of Company Secretaries of India (ICSI), and the Institute of Cost and Management Accountants of India (ICMAI), Mr. Mittal exemplifies dedication and excellence in his fields.

Hailing from the village of Danta in Sikar district, Rajasthan, Mr. Mittal embarked on his journey to Kolkata with a strong sense of purpose. He established his businesses from the ground up, guiding them to significant growth and eventually to a successful IPO, creating substantial value along the way.

Beyond his entrepreneurial accomplishments, Mr. Mittal has a deeply philanthropic spirit. He founded Tree Campus Academy, a social initiative dedicated to teaching English to Hindi and

Bengali speakers through a user-friendly app and online classes, empowering individuals with essential language skills. He also serves as a founding trustee of the Microsec Foundation, working to make a positive impact on society.

At the core of Mr. Mittal's philosophy lies a commitment to 'Being Genuine', a value he holds dearly, along with a joyful approach to life, embodying the spirit of 'Being Child'. His journey is a testament to his unwavering dedication to both business innovation and social betterment.

You can connect with him at blmittal@sastasundar.com